Nomadic Mindset

The Future of Digital Work

by

Lisa Thompson

Table of Contents

Introduction

Imagine the sun warming your skin as you tap away at your laptop, the gentle lapping of the ocean's waves providing the perfect backdrop to your workday. This image, once a far-off fantasy, is today a tangible reality for an ever-growing tribe of professionals who have dared to rewrite the rules of the nine-to-five grind. Welcome to the era of the digital nomad, a movement that is reshaping the very fabric of work and life as we know it.

The digital nomad lifestyle is about more than just exotic locales and Instagram-worthy coffee shops. It represents a seismic shift in our understanding of how careers can be built and nurtured. No longer confined by the four walls of an office, individuals across the globe are harnessing the power of technology to carve out professional paths that offer freedom, flexibility, and fulfillment.

This book isn't just a guide; it's a compass for navigating the dynamic landscape of remote work. As we delve into the world of digital nomadism, we dissect the allure of a boundary-less life and lay bare the challenges that come with it. But beyond that, we seek to kindle in you a spirit of adventure and adaptability that is critical to thrive in this ever-evolving work paradigm.

Our journey together begins with untangling the intricacies of the nomadic mindset. What drives someone to unmoor from the stability of traditional employment? How does one adapt to the uncertainty that accompanies a life in motion? Understanding these underpinnings sets the stage for a successful transition into digital nomadism.

Next, we define what it truly means to be a digital nomad. It's a term that's thrown around with abandon these days, but we'll get to the heart of it, examining not just the how, but the why. Unpacking the psychological, technological, and geographical components that constitute this lifestyle will empower you to assess your own readiness for the journey ahead.

Equipping yourself with the right tools is imperative, and Chapter 3 is your toolkit. From identifying online platforms that enable remote work to selecting the best apps for productivity and communication, we'll ensure you're well-prepared to tackle professional challenges, no matter where you are in the world.

But it's not enough to pack your digital toolbox; a meticulously crafted plan for your transition into nomadism is vital. In Chapter 4, we provide a roadmap for establishing goals, expectations, and a balanced approach to integrating work with the wonders of wanderlust. This isn't about taking a leap into the unknown—it's about setting a sustainable pace for your new lifestyle.

As you venture forth, building a remote career that aligns with your passion and skills is non-negotiable. We'll explore the remote job market, highlighting in-demand digital roles and emphasizing the importance of continuous learning. Networking and personal branding in this space can be distinct, and we'll offer insights on mastering these facets to boost your visibility and opportunities.

Logistical hurdles can't be overlooked; Chapter 6 tackles the nitty-gritty of legalities, financial planning, and establishing a virtual base. We'll demystify visas, taxes, insurance, and other essentials, ensuring you're prepared for the practicalities of nomadic life.

Yet, even the best-laid plans can be besieged by obstacles. Chapter 7 addresses head-on the realities of isolation, burnout, and unexpected challenges. Through proven strategies and community support, you can navigate these waters and maintain your mental health and well-being.

A global mindset isn't just advantageous; it's imperative. Cultivating sensitivity to cultural nuances and learning how to adapt to diverse settings will enrich your experience and foster an empathetic approach to life and work—a theme we'll delve deeply into in Chapter 8.

The digital nomad movement isn't happening in a vacuum. In Chapter 9, we consider the broader implications on society, including the future of urban spaces and the environmental impact of this lifestyle. Remote work isn't just changing how we live; it's changing the world around us.

What lies ahead for digital nomadism? Chapter 10 peers into the crystal ball, evaluating market trends and technological advancements that could further transform this way of working and living. Being ahead of the curve will place you in a position of advantage as you navigate the future of work.

Lest you think this is all theory, Chapter 11 brings you heartfelt stories from those who are living the dream. Their triumphs and trials paint a realistic picture of what it means to be a digital nomad and serve as both warnings and inspiration for your own expedition.

Lastly, leaving a mark in this transient lifestyle is about building a legacy. In Chapter 12, we discuss personal branding and how you can engage with and share your journey in meaningful ways, leaving behind digital footprints that resonate with others and echo your values long after you've moved on to your next destination.

With every chapter, you'll gain insights and actionable steps that will equip you to transition into, or flourish within, digital nomadism. This lifestyle is a manifestation of freedom and self-determination in the digital age, a spirited pursuit of work and pleasure without compromising one for the other.

Join us on this odyssey, and push beyond the boundaries of conventional employment. Embrace the complexities, the liberations, and the rich tapestry of experiences that await you as a digital nomad. It's time to chart your course, expand your horizons, and redefine what it means to live and work in harmony with the world. Your adventure starts here.

Chapter 1
Unveiling the Nomadic Mindset

Prying open the nomadic mindset is akin to stepping into a vast, borderless expanse where every horizon promises a new adventure and a lesson in self-discovery. This mindset is an intricate tapestry of resilience, curiosity, and the unwavering belief that life is not meant to be lived in one place. Today's digital nomads aren't just bucking the trend; they're rewriting the script of conventional work-life, weaving flexibility and freedom into their professional narratives. Let's peel back the layers, revealing how years of shifting workplace dynamics and tech innovations have culminated in this cultural renaissance that champions mobility and remote careers. As the first echoes of the nomadic future resonate within you, remember: the journey ahead isn't just a change in scenery, but a transformation that reshapes one's essence—unlocking potential, bridging continents, and constructing the latticework of a globally intertwined community. Embrace this initial step of understanding the nomadic mindset; it is the cornerstone of a life less ordinary, built upon the ever-shifting sands of personal growth and professional ingenuity.

The Evolution of Work

As we embark on this unfolding narrative of the nomadic mindset, let's pause and consider the metamorphosis of work—a dramatic shift from the rigidity of yesteryears to today's free-flowing gig economy. Picture this: just a few decades ago, the workday shuffle featured a predictable soundtrack, footsteps echoing in tiled corridors leading to rows of cubicles, a sea of suits, and the clacking of typewriters. Now, replace that scene with the soft hum of a coffee shop, laptops aglow with ambition, and faces lit by the promise of a Skype call closing the deal from a beach in Bali. This evolution has ripped up the rulebook and rewritten it with flexibility, autonomy, and a pinch of adventure. It has set the stage for the digital nomad—intrepid spirits who navigate the digital oceans with skill, harnessing the winds of technological advancement to break away from the anchor of traditional office spaces. And in this section, we'll dive deep into this evolution, understanding how the roots of work have spread into every corner of our lives, reshaping what it means to earn a living and challenging us to redefine success on our own terms.

From Cubicles to Cafes: A Historical Perspective Let's embark on a journey through time to trace the transformative path from the traditional office cubicles that once defined our working lives to the informal, flexible cafes that have become the new frontier for the modern workforce. This transformation marks more than just a change of scenery; it's a profound shift in our work culture and the very essence of what it means to be professionally engaged.

The structured, monolithic office spaces of the late 20th century were originally born from a desire for efficiency, order, and a tight control over the working environment. Rows of identical cubicles aimed to maximize space usage while minimizing distractions, embodying the industrial spirit that work was serious business requiring rigid boundaries and stern discipline.

But as technology advanced, those gray walls began to feel less like a structure supporting productivity and more like a barrier to creativity and human interaction. A latent hunger grew among the workforce for autonomy, meaningful work, and, importantly, the freedom to choose one's own working environment. The days of clocking in and out at the same time, wearing a suit, and sitting beneath fluorescent lights began to feel archaic.

The dawn of the internet in the mid-90s sparked an unheralded revolution – the beginnings of a digital globalization that gradually untethered many of us from the need to physically be in an office. With the arrival of the new millennium, the seeds of remote work were firmly planted, and they began to take root in the fertile soil of an increasingly connected world.

Fuelled by this newfound connectivity, the coffee shop emerged as a symbol of this budding work-culture paradigm. As if overnight, cafes across cities began to hum with the clatter of keyboards and the murmurs of Skype calls. A generation of freelancers and entrepreneurs made the cafe their office, drawn by the scent of fresh coffee, the casual ambiance, and the promise of human connection.

This wasn't just a trend, it signaled a fundamental shift. Flexibility wasn't only desirable; it became synonymous with a new form of productivity that wasn't measured by hours spent in a chair but by actual output and results. A realization dawned that work could, in fact, be done from anywhere, and this liberated thousands from the constraints of the cubicle.

The explosion of the gig economy and platforms that connect freelancers with clients globally only added fuel to the fire of this workplace evolution. Now, not only could you work from anywhere, but you could also work for anyone. Geographical boundaries melted away, as did the traditional 9-to-5 workday.

As the 21st century progressed, a new term entered our lexicon: "digital nomadism." It encompassed those who took remote work to the next level, not just stepping out of the office but also stepping into the world. These pioneers took the concept of the cafe as an office and expanded it to beaches, mountainsides, and cities around the globe.

Companies too began to see the light, recognizing that happy employees are productive employees, and happiness often equated to autonomy and flexibility. Tech giants started to offer remote work options, and slowly, traditional businesses followed suit, realizing that they could tap into a worldwide talent pool and reduce their overhead costs in the process.

Critical to this evolution was the development of co-working spaces, the hybrid between an office and a cafe. These hubs of creativity and collaboration sprouted in cities worldwide, offering not just desks but a community. A home away from home (and the cubicle) for innovators, visionaries, and anyone who sought to redefine the meaning of work.

However, this shift didn't just affect where we work but also how we work. Coworking spaces and cafes encourage networking and shared learning, breaking down corporate silos and fostering a culture of shared success. As ideas freely circulated in these new environments, they sparked new ventures and collaborations that would've been unimaginable within the insular walls of traditional offices.

Naturally, as with any tectonic shift, the transition from structured offices to more fluid workspaces wasn't seamless. It required — and still does — a methodical unravelling of deeply ingrained notions of professionalism, a redefinition of what it means to be "at work." The early adopters faced skepticism and the challenge of proving that productivity isn't location-dependent.

And within this transformation lies a profound lesson: adaptability is key. As remote work technology continues to advance and as our society becomes ever more mobile, it's those who can adapt to new ways of working, new ways of thinking, and new ways of living who will thrive. Embracing the uncertainty, adapting to the ever-changing work landscape, and finding joy in the flexibility is the essence of being a digital nomad.

The passage from cubicles to cafes, then, is about more than the abandonment of physical office space. It's about the rejection of the one-size-fits-all model of work in favor of something personalized, something that fits the life you choose to live. It's about harnessing the power of technology not to tether us to a desk, but to free us from it. So, here's to finding your own corner of the world – in a buzzing cafe or a tranquil beach – and making it your own stage for professional success.

What began as a ripple in the pond of the work world has become a wave. To ride this wave, to be a part of this immense shift, is to be at the helm of your destiny. So set sail from the safe harbor of the cubicle and navigate the vibrant, uncharted waters of cafes, co-working spaces, and the world beyond. This is the historical backdrop against which your story as a digital nomad will unfold.

The Rise of the Digital Nomad Imagine waking to the gentle lapping of waves on a sun-kissed shore, your laptop a portal to clients, colleagues, and communities that span across continents. This isn't just a daydream; it's the reality for an ever-growing tribe of workers who've cast off the chains of conventional office life and embraced the digital nomad lifestyle.

What's sparked this grand exodus from the traditional workspace? A confluence of technology, timing, and a burgeoning sense of wanderlust. As high-speed internet becomes ubiquitous and the tether to physical office spaces loosens, a surge of individuals are seizing the chance to merge life and work in a seamless, adventurous blend.

But, let's not get ahead of ourselves. To fully appreciate the movement that has led many to trade in their desk chairs for hammocks, a little context is in order. The digital nomad phenomenon isn't an overnight fad; it's the culmination of a gradual shift towards remote working models, spearheaded by technologies that empower us to communicate and collaborate from virtually anywhere.

At the core of this paradigm shift is a desire for freedom and flexibility. People are increasingly asking for more control over their time and location, rebelling against what they see as an outdated model that ties value to a physical presence in an office. And as companies become more receptive to these demands, the path to a nomadic lifestyle becomes less rocky.

One might wonder, who embodies the archetype of a digital nomad? Is it the tech whiz coding from a beach in Bali, the freelance writer drafting articles from a cafe in Paris, or the consultant strategizing from a mountaintop in Peru? It's all of these and more. The beauty of digital nomadism is that it doesn't discriminate by profession but is unified by a shared longing for autonomy.

Alongside the allure of exploration and self-directed living comes the shrewd business sense that pervades the digital nomad community. Nomads aren't just drifting leisurely from place to place; they're making strategic decisions about cost of living, Wi-Fi reliability, and local entrepreneurial ecosystems, transforming cities and towns across the globe into hotbeds of innovation and creativity.

However, let's not don rose-tinted glasses. The digital nomad lifestyle is not without its hurdles. It requires a blend of self-discipline, savvy planning, and the resilience to face loneliness, instability, and the occasional Wi-Fi outage. But those who navigate these challenges are often rewarded with enriched lives, filled with diverse experiences that far outweigh the comforts of routine.

The internet's role in this transformation cannot be understated. With a bounty of tools and platforms at their disposal, digital nomads can maintain productivity, manage their finances, and build communities that provide support and camaraderie, all within the digital realm.

And so, we find ourselves at a tipping point. Digital nomadism is no longer a fringe lifestyle but a viable, even enviable, way of working and living. The rise of collaborative technology, co-working spaces, and a global emphasis on work-life integration push this trend from the margins to the mainstream.

We're witnessing a redefinition of what it means to be a worker, or more aptly, a professional human. No longer confined, we're watching a generation redefine work in a way that brings satisfaction, balance, and a touch of the extraordinary into daily life—and it's happening on a scale we've never seen before.

So, let's take a moment to reflect. If the 9-to-5 mold feels like a straitjacket, stifling your potential and dulling your experiences, know that there's another path unfurling before you. The rise of the digital nomad offers a blueprint for a life less ordinary, crafted on the tenets of connectivity, autonomy, and perpetual growth.

Perhaps you're teetering on the edge of joining this modern migration. You're armed with skills and a thirst for something greater than what lies within cubicle walls. The digital nomadic lifestyle whispers of possibilities that extend beyond the horizon, of a workday that aligns with your values, aspirations, and love for discovery.

The rise of the digital nomad is more than a mere trend; it's a cultural shift that reimagines the intersection of work, life, and geography. It's a movement for those brave enough to question the status quo and bold enough to craft a life that resonates with their innermost desires.

Intrigued? You're not alone. Across the world, individuals are packing their bags and laptops, leaping into a life that promises as much uncertainty as it does reward. They are the digital nomads, and their number is rising. Tomorrow's workers won't be asking for a window office; they'll be working from anywhere, their office views as variable as the weather. And you? You could be one of them.

With each chapter of this book, you'll edge closer to that reality. We'll deep dive into the mechanics, the mindset, and the magic of being a digital nomad. So let's journey together, learning, adapting, and embracing the winds of change as we explore what it means to be truly, wonderfully, nomadic.

Chapter 2:
Defining Digital Nomadism

Imagine embracing the liberty to venture across terrains while your laptop hums softly with work's ebb and flow—that's the essence of digital nomadism. It's more than a buzzword; it's a paradigm shift in our very approach to balancing life and livelihood. At its core, a nomadic lifestyle fuses the power of technology with the innate human craving for exploration and autonomy. This chapter peels back the layers to reveal not just what this trend encapsulates, but the why's and how's it's redefining professional landscapes. We delve into the spirit of being a nomad—shedding light on the digital tools and freedoms that form its backbone, and the psychological tapestry that often goes unseen yet shapes every part of this modern expedition. Empowerment kicks in when you're clued into the digital wizardry that enables seamless connection from any nook of the world, and geographic independence becomes your trump card in this life-sized game of chess. So, let's dissect this lifestyle, understanding its DNA, and prepare you to weave your own nomadic narrative, full of resolve, resilience, and the romance of rendezvous with the unknown.

The Key Components of a Nomadic Lifestyle

Painting the canvas of a nomadic lifestyle involves a fusion of freedom and strategy, where resourcefulness and flexibility are the bristles that bring this portrait to life. Think of it as a drop-down menu of your life where you're constantly selecting new coordinates for both your WiFi signal and your window view. You'll be swapping the static comfort zone for an ever-evolving adventure, with technology as your trusty sidekick. This lifestyle isn't just about tossing a few belongings into a backpack; it's about transforming the day-to-day into a harmonized rhythm of work and exploration. In essence, the key components of a nomadic lifestyle are the seamless integration of productivity, movement, and the ability to thrive in a state of constant change. And that's just the surface. You'll also curate resilience like a master, mastering the balancing act between wanderlust and deadlines, all while etching your digital footprint across continents.

Technological Empowerment as a digital nomad is not just about having the latest gadgets; it's a crucial pillar supporting the entire nomadic lifestyle. It's about harnessing technology to create a seamless blend of work and wanderlust. Imagine possessing the ability to transform any corner of the world into your office, all thanks to the power at your fingertips. That's the heartbeat of the nomadic lifestyle.

One thing's for sure, the digital revolution has leveled the playing field. No matter if you're in Bali or Barcelona, if you've got a reliable internet connection and the right set of tools, you can compete with the best in business. The internet is your gateway to global markets and remote work opportunities that allow you to live life on your own terms. But what exactly does it take to be technologically empowered?

First off, let's talk about connectivity. It's the lifeblood of remote work. Without it, you're basically stranded. Therefore, an empowered nomad understands the necessity of a solid, fast, and secure internet connection. They'll have backup plans, like a global data plan or a portable Wi-Fi device. There's nothing more empowering than knowing you can connect to your team or clients without skipping a beat, no matter where you're exploring.

The next piece of the tech puzzle is hardware. Lightweight laptops, durable smartphones, and noise-cancelling headphones are the tools that facilitate digital mastery. Selecting devices that balance portability with performance is key. They must withstand the knocks and bumps of travel while offering enough juice to power through your tasks.

Software and apps fuel efficiency and productivity for digital nomads. From project management tools like Asana or Trello to communication platforms like Slack and Zoom, these are the conduits through which work flows smoothly. Mastery over these tools isn't optional; it's essential. It allows for coordination with clients or teams half a world away, and empowers nomads to stay aligned with various time zones and work schedules.

Cloud services, such as Google Drive or Dropbox, are equally significant. These platforms allow you to access and share your work from anywhere. No more panic about leaving a crucial file on a USB stick in a café. With everything stored safely in the cloud, you can breathe easy knowing that your work travels with you, securely and conveniently.

Empowerment also comes from knowledge. Understanding the basics of cybersecurity and how to protect your data is critical. A seasoned digital nomad is savvy about using VPNs to maintain privacy and securing devices with strong passwords and encryption. They know that safeguarding intellectual property and personal information isn't just smart; it's non-negotiable.

Financial technology has revolutionized the way nomads handle money. With fintech solutions like TransferWise, PayPal, and a host of banking apps, managing finances across borders is no longer a headache. Getting paid, accessing funds, or tracking expenses can now be done with a few taps on your phone, keeping you financially empowered and focused on your work and travel.

Online learning platforms are the unsung heroes of the nomadic lifestyle. Places like Coursera, Udemy, and LinkedIn Learning ensure that you keep your skills razor-sharp. Whether it's coding, design, marketing, or a new language, these resources guarantee that your professional development doesn't miss a beat while you're globe-trotting.

It's not just about working; technology also simplifies the travel aspect of nomadism. From Airbnb to Skyscanner, the savvy nomad leverages these tools to find accommodations and flights, often scoring the best deals. These apps don't just save you money; they save you something equally valuable: time.

But remember, it's not all sunshine and sandy beaches. Tech can fail, and an empowered nomad is always prepared for when it does. This means having offline resources available, whether that's e-books or downloaded work, so that a glitch doesn't derail your entire day. A versatile mindset and a plan B are your best tools when things go sideways.

Your personal brand is also a critical component of your digital presence, and technology is the megaphone. Social media platforms are the stages on which you broadcast your professional narrative. Platforms like LinkedIn, Instagram, and Medium allow you to share your story, showcasing your skills, and establishing you as a thought leader in your field.

Meanwhile, digital marketing tools like Google Analytics, SEMrush, and Mailchimp provide insights and reach, allowing you to measure the impact of your work and adjust accordingly. An empowered nomad knows the power of data and uses it to optimize their output, ensuring they're hitting the right notes with their audience.

Automation and AI are more than just buzzwords for the forward-thinking nomad; they're efficiency boosters. Automating repetitive tasks with apps like Zapier or IFTTT gives you back time to focus on high-value tasks or to explore your latest destination. It's about working smarter, not just harder.

Lastly, an empowered nomad stays connected to the heartbeat of innovation, keeping an eye on emerging technologies. Whether it's the rise of blockchain, the potential of virtual reality for remote collaboration, or the future of AI in the workplace, staying informed means staying ahead. It's about being adaptable and ready to ride the wave of the next big thing.

As much as technology revolutionizes the work aspect, it also brings nomads together. Online forums, social groups, and virtual meetups empower you to connect with others on similar journeys, exchange tips, share work opportunities, and even collaborate. The sense of community that technology fosters can be a lifeline in moments of solitude or when you're seeking advice.

So, think of technological empowerment not just as a means to work remotely but as the very essence that breathes life into the digital nomad lifestyle. It's the thread that weaves together productivity, connectivity, learning, and community. With technology as your ally, the world isn't just your oyster—it's your office, your classroom, and your playground.

Geographic Independence: Imagine waking up to the soft golden hues of sunrise not from your usual bedroom window, but from a quaint beachside hut in Bali. Later, a tap on your laptop summons up work from a different time zone, while waves murmur approval at your latest venture. This isn't a whimsical daydream, but a chapter from the life of a digital nomad who's unlocked the key aspect of their lifestyle: geographic independence.

Geographic independence is the linchpin of digital nomadism. It's seeing the world not as a string of vacation spots but potential offices. Under the canopy of geographic independence, you curate a lifestyle where your income doesn't tie you down to a specific location; rather, it offers a world where borders blur in professional significance. Your career transforms into a vessel that lets you explore, learn, and grow—both personally and professionally.

Empowerment comes hand in hand with choosing your coordinates on the map. Whether you're sipping a latte in a bustling European city, or taking a conference call from a hammock in the Caribbean, it's about where you feel most productive, inspired, and balanced. This freedom is intoxicating, but remember, it's driven by responsibility. The discipline to work when no one's watching, and the action to stop working when the whole world beckons.

With this autonomy, you'll find that routines are not constraints, but rhythms you set to the beat of your own drum. Maybe you're an early riser, coding as the roosters crow, or perhaps a night owl, creating marketing strategies under the stars. Geographic independence means reshaping the 9-to-5 format to fit the highs and lows of your creative ebb and flow, regardless of the zip code.

However, let's not mistake this for endless globetrotting without pause. Embrace slow travel—immerse yourself in communities, understand the local fabric, and savor experiences over a period that allows roots to form, even if they're temporary. The profound cultural insights, the relationships fostered, and the skill of blending into new ecosystems are as valuable as your professional output.

Managing clients and projects can be challenging with varying time zones, but it unlocks a new realm of possibilities. You're now in a position to work with clients across continents, sourcing global opportunities and charging rates that reflect the universal value of your skills. A well-timed schedule and clear communication can turn what seems like a hurdle into a strategic advantage.

As you navigate through the waves of global freelancing or remote employment, keep your sails directed towards financial security. Geographic independence isn't about escaping monetary reality, it's about smartly crafting a stable income flow that can withstand currency fluctuations and economic variations of your chosen locales.

Dabble in the local flavors—both metaphorically and literally. Get a taste of local cuisines, incorporate regional aesthetics into your creative endeavors, or bring local business practices into your portfolio. Let your work be a bridge between cultures while maintaining a responsible and sustainable approach to your presence in these places.

Developing a robust network while on the move is essential. Geographic independence doesn't equate to societal isolation. Forge connections in coworking spaces, attend local meetups, and use social platforms to deepen bonds. These connections can lead to collaborations, future projects, or simply enrich your nomadic experience with shared stories and laughs.

Be mindful that geographic independence necessitates a unique blend of flexibility and structure. While your office view can change as often as the tides, ensure that your productivity and output remain consistent. Clients and colleagues rely on your professionalism; hence systems, routines, and a solid work ethic must travel in your suitcase alongside your gadgets and gear.

Security is paramount. Equip yourself with the necessary knowledge about healthcare, insurance, and emergency procedures in every new destination. The thrill of new horizons is best enjoyed with a safety net firmly in place, enabling you to pursue adventure without reckless abandon.

It's not merely about wandering the globe; it's thriving while doing so. Geographic independence means setting up shop wherever you lay your hat, developing a keen sense for good workspots, and always seeking out that perfect balance between comfort, curiosity, and productivity. Imagine transforming any corner of the world into a space that fuels your passion and feeds your soul.

Celebrate the beauty of a transient lifestyle and the learning that comes from each new move. Let go of the possessions that anchor you unnecessarily and cultivate possessions that matter—experiences, skills, memories. These are the true companions of a digital nomad, the real treasures that cross borders seamlessly and enrich far beyond the tangible.

Wrapping up the mosaic of geographic independence, remember that this chapter in your life will be one of profound personal development. Every new zip code is a classroom, every local interaction, a lesson. Engage fully with the culture and the environment, and watch as your worldview expands in sync with the stamps decorating your passport.

Geographic independence is more than a feature of being a digital nomad—it's a testament to the human spirit's adaptability and drive for freedom. It's a call to discover not just the planet's hidden corners but also the depths of your own capabilities. It beckons you to redefine what it means to live and work, turning the whole world into a backdrop for your personal and professional evolution.

The Psychology of the Nomad

Nomadic living is not merely a shift in geography or a new approach to work; it's a profound transformation of one's inner landscape. The mind of a digital nomad is wired differently; certain traits and perspectives are not just beneficial but necessary for thriving on this unconventional path. Let's explore the psychological makeup of a digital nomad and what it takes to embrace this lifestyle wholeheartedly.

Firstly, nomads are naturally curious beings. A sense of wonder leads them to unknown corners of the world and into novel professional opportunities. This curiosity, fueled by an insatiable desire to learn and grow, is what keeps a nomad moving forward, even when the journey gets tough.

Adaptability is another pillar of the nomadic psyche. As one's environment is ever-changing, so must be one's ability to adjust and morph with new circumstances and cultures. The successful digital nomad doesn't resist change; they ride its waves with an unwavering belief that evolution is part of the journey.

Resilience needs to be woven into the nomad's very fabric. There will be setbacks and discomforts. It's not a question of if, but when. Resilience isn't just about bouncing back; it's about learning and integrating those lessons into future adventures.

Independence is also at the core of nomadic psychology. The autonomy to carve your own path is intoxicating but requires a strong sense of self and an unwavering trust in one's abilities. Digital nomads must be their own anchor in an ocean of uncertainty.

Risk tolerance is often high among digital nomads. They see potential where others see peril and are willing to leap into the void with the confidence that they'll land on their feet—or at least, know how to roll when they hit the ground.

A digital nomad's life involves constant learning. A dedication to personal and professional development is crucial. Whether it's mastering a new digital tool or picking up a few phrases in a foreign language, growth is part of the daily routine.

Communication skills are vital, too. While nomads may wander physically, they must remain connected with clients, colleagues, and the broader community. They know how to articulate their ideas and listen actively, regardless of the medium.

The urge for meaningful experiences propels the nomad forward. Every stamp in their passport, every job completed from a far-flung locale adds to the richness of their life's tapestry. Purpose drives them more than mere profit.

Patience, though not always a virtue associated with adventurous spirits, is critical. Wifi may falter, bureaucracy can slow plans, but a nomad knows that frustration is a detour, not a dead-end. By playing the long game, they often come out ahead.

Self-awareness allows nomads to understand their limits and boundaries. By knowing when they need a break or when it's time to push harder, they can manage their energy and maintain their wellbeing on the road.

Emotional intelligence goes hand-in-hand with self-awareness. Nomads must be adept at recognizing and regulating their emotions and deciphering those of others, especially when crossing cultural boundaries.

Confidence is the bedrock upon which the nomadic life is built. With each successful adaptation, problem solved, and connection made, the nomad's self-belief grows, fueling further ventures into the unknown.

Intuition often guides nomads through the unpredictable landscape of their lifestyle. Sometimes, it's that quiet voice inside that nudges them to take one road over another or to trust a new acquaintance.

Sustainability is a pervasive theme in the psyche of the long-term nomad. Quick fixes and short-term thinking are replaced with strategies for long-term success, be it financial health, personal relationships, or environmental impact.

Finally, gratitude is a touchstone for the digital nomad. They appreciate the freedoms afforded by their lifestyle, the people they meet, the lessons learned, and the beauty of the world around them. This sense of gratitude keeps their spirits high and their feet grounded, no matter where their travels take them.

Embracing these psychological aspects doesn't happen overnight, but rather through the ongoing, vibrant dance of experiences and introspection. Understanding and nurturing these traits within yourself can pave the way to building a fulfilling and sustainable life as a digital nomad.

Chapter 3:
Tools of the Trade

Laying the groundwork for a life untethered starts with armory - not of weapons, but of gadgets and apps that keep you connected and productive across time zones and latitudes. We can't talk about the digital nomad lifestyle without a nod to the digital arsenal that makes it all possible. Your tech kit is as crucial to your survival as your passport. It's about striking that sweet spot between power and portability, ensuring you've got the hardware to hammer out work from a hammock or hack growth strategies from a high-speed train. But it's not just hardware; it's also the mesh of apps and platforms that link you to clients, clout, and colleagues. Communication tools and productivity systems become the lifeblood of your workflow, the silent partners in your globetrotting enterprise. This chapter doesn't just list essentials; it empowers you to pick the right tech sherpa for your journey and tailor your toolkit, so you're never at a disadvantage, whether you're dialing into a conference call from a beach bungalow or delivering a pitch from a mountain retreat. Embrace these tools, and you've got more than a fighting chance to thrive anywhere on this blue marble of ours.

Essential Digital Resources

As we gear up for the grand voyage into the world of digital nomadism, it's imperative to pack the virtual suitcase with the right tools. Imagine this: you're not just packing your favorite jeans; you're meticulously selecting the tech essentials that will fuel your remote career and sustain your wanderlust. We're talking about an arsenal of digital resources that complement the fluid, boundary-less lifestyle you're about to embrace. This is where we dive deep into the heartbeat of a digital nomad's existence—the platforms, apps, and software that streamline workflow and maintain productivity against the backdrop of ever-changing time zones. Can you feel the empowerment buzzing through your fingertips as you harness the power of cloud-based services, collaborative tools, and communication wonders that make the world your office? Nailing the right set of digital resources isn't just conducive to success; it's the lifeline that connects you to clients and communities across the globe, ensuring you can thrive professionally while feasting on the freedom of life beyond the conventional desk.

Leveraging Online Platforms for Work Imagine the vast expanse of the digital ecosystem as your new office. It's not just a place; it's a space where opportunities are boundless and where your career can take flight without you ever having to leave your favorite coffee shop. In this section, we're dialing into how you can harness the power of online platforms to not just work remotely, but to thrive in the digital nomad landscape.

The first truth you've got to embrace is that online platforms are the pillars of modern remote work. Just like traditional occupations rely on bricks and mortar to host their businesses, digital nomads depend on virtual real estate. Platforms like Upwork, LinkedIn, and Fiverr have become the cornerstones of finding and securing remote work. Each one offers a unique environment to showcase your skills and connect with clients worldwide.

Let's slice into Upwork like it's a juicy piece of opportunity pie. It's a phenomenal starting point, especially if you're new to the freelancing jungle. With millions of jobs posted annually across a kaleidoscope of fields, diving into Upwork can often mean the difference between a nomadic dream and a nomadic reality. Tailor your profile to stand out, highlight your niche skills, and always, always personalize your proposals!

LinkedIn, the professional network giant, is your digital handshake. It's not just for job searches; it's a platform to establish your brand. Engage with content, share your experiences, and use its robust job search functionality. The trick here is to be authentic and proactive. Connect with industry leaders, comment on discussions, and make your presence felt.

Fiverr flips the script by having clients come to you. Set up your 'Gig,' establish your packages, and wait for the bite. But the key here is to be patient and consistent. High-quality service leads to positive reviews which, in turn, lead to more clients. It's a snowball of success just waiting to roll.

But the journey doesn't end with freelancing platforms. Blogging has stood the test of time as an online work catalyst. Create value through your content, monetize your website with affiliate marketing, sponsored content, or memberships. A blog is a stage for your voice and can establish you as an authority in your niche.

What can't be overlooked is the rise of teaching and tutoring platforms. Teaching English online has helped countless nomads sustain their travels. But why stop there? Platforms like Teachable allow you to create courses on anything from web development to yoga, empowering you to earn while sharing knowledge.

Oh, and let's not forget about the creative powerhouses - Etsy for the crafters, Behance for the designers, and Patreon for just about anything creative under the sun. These platforms empower artistry and originality, enabling you to sell unique goods and services directly to your audience.

Software development, a cornerstone of the digital economy, has coding playgrounds like GitHub and Stack Overflow. Contribute to projects, showcase your portfolio, and before you know it, you're in demand for your programming prowess.

Remember that each platform, each app, each website, is just a tool. Their effectiveness depends entirely on how you wield them. Engage in strategic networking. Your next big gig could come from a comment you left on a forum, or a tweet that sparked a conversation. Being active in digital communities relevant to your niche can put you onto the radar of clients and collaborators alike.

As with any tool, you must stay sharp. Continually refine your skills through online courses and webinars. Platforms change, algorithms update, new apps emerge. Keeping abreast of these changes and adapting your strategy accordingly is what will keep your nomadic career on the upward trajectory.

But what happens when you face a saturated market? Stand out by building a robust portfolio that speaks to the quality of your work. Use platforms like Medium to publish thought leadership pieces, or GitHub to contribute to trending projects. Your active presence and quality contributions become your differentiation point.

Don't overlook the smaller, niche platforms either. Sometimes, these can be goldmines for specialized work and have communities that value quality and specialization over quantity. Networks like Dribbble for designers or Toptal for finance professionals can be less crowded, offering greater visibility for your skills.

Ride the wave of social media as well. Platforms like Instagram and TikTok can be potent tools for visual storytellers and influencers. And remember, as platforms evolve, so do the possibilities they present. Live streaming, for example, has opened up new avenues for engagement and monetization.

To truly leverage online platforms, you must be both the master and the apprentice—always learning, always evolving. The moment you stagnate is the moment opportunities pass you by. So, stay curious and be relentless in your quest for growth.

To wrap it up, consider this: the world of online work is like a constantly shifting mosaic. You have the power to arrange the pieces to create your masterpiece of a nomadic career. Equip yourself with the knowledge of platforms, present yourself with charisma and competence, and prepare for an exhilarating journey on the digital highway toward independence and global connectivity.

The Digital Nomad's Tech Kit Embracing the nomadic lifestyle isn't just about slapping a laptop sticker that reads "adventure" across the back of your screen. The true essence of digital nomadism lies within the veins of technology that allow you to connect and create from any corner of the globe. Imagine setting up your 'office' with a view of the majestic Andes or while listening to the waves of the Indian Ocean - it's all possible with the right tech kit.

First and foremost, let's talk laptops. This gatekeeper to the digital world needs to be robust yet lightweight, with enough juice to keep you tethered to your tasks without having to hunt for an outlet every few hours. Battery life becomes your new best friend. And don't overlook the power of a good processor and solid-state drive; efficiency is king in the realm of remote work.

Speaking of efficiency, can we just take a moment to appreciate the life-changing magic of a reliable cloud service? Whether you're team Google Drive, Dropbox, or any other, the ability to access and share your files from anywhere is nothing short of wizardry. Keep your documents, presentations, and spreadsheets at your fingertips, because nothing smacks unprofessionalism like "Sorry, that file's on my other computer."

Connectivity is the lifeblood of digital nomadism. A mobile hotspot device is a must-have for those times when Wi-Fi is as elusive as a mirage in the desert. Couple that with a virtual private network (VPN) service to keep your connections secure and frequent flier stress at bay. After all, there's nothing quaint about cyber threats or inaccessible websites due to geographic restrictions.

Next, consider the sheer convenience of a good pair of noise-cancelling headphones. These do not just block out the drone of engines or coffee shop chatter, they're a universal "do not disturb" sign when you're in the zone. Plus, when you're ready to unwind, they bring the soothing tunes or podcasts that transform any foreign room into a slice of home.

A reliable power bank is another crucial addition to your tech arsenal. When wandering off the beaten path (literally), these portable powerhouses ensure you don't miss a beat—or an important client call—simply because you opted for an impromptu jungle trek.

But what about those cumbersome tasks that touchscreens fumble? Enter the portable keyboard and mouse duo. Lightweight and compact, they are the unsung heroes that restore your ergonomic sanity. A foldable keyboard and an optical mouse can turn any flat surface into a proper workstation.

Tablets have also found their sweet spot among the nomadic tribe. Ideal for reading, quick browsing, or as a second screen when multi-tasking, they bridge the gap between phone and laptop, proving that sometimes, the middle child does get it right.

Let's not forget the often-overlooked but ever-essential, surge protector. Far from the most glamorous of gadgets, its value is realized the moment a sudden voltage spike threatens to fry your main source of income. Think of it as a guardian angel for your gadgets.

Subtle but mighty, a good-quality external hard drive or SSD offers another layer of backup for the meticulous nomad. Because sometimes, the cloud isn't enough, and you need the reassuring solidity of extra storage you can hold in your palm.

While we're discussing backups, let's talk multifunctional travel adapters. Not just because you need to plug in, but because in a world where one size never fits all, these adapters are the diplomats smoothing over the compatibility issues between your devices and the numerous plug types you'll encounter.

Remember, it's not just about owning these gadgets, but also about learning the most efficient ways to use them. Maximizing battery life, wrangling file formats, and a host of keyboard shortcuts becomes part of your intangible toolkit. The digital nomad is both artist and artisan, where their craft relies as much on the paint as the stroke of their brush.

As much as we've embraced the wireless world, don't underestimate the power of a few well-chosen cables. A durable USB-C or lightning cable can be a lifeline in a pinch, and managing them with organizers or clips is a small habit that prevents big tangles and frustrations.

And for those moments when inspiration strikes under the stars or the deadline beckons despite a blackout, an LED USB light can be a game-changer. Directly plugged into your laptop, it disperses enough glow to keep the keys—and your ideas—illuminated.

To cap it off, consider every tech piece an extension of your professionalself. Keep them clean, updated, and in good repair. Your presentation to the world isn't just about a crisp shirt or a firm handshake anymore—it's reflected in the wellness of your Wi-Fi signal and the readiness of your RAM.

So there you have it, an insider's scoop on crafting the ultimate tech kit, the constant companions on your journey. These are the tools that empower you to achieve that coveted work-life synergy, where productivity meets freedom, making the entire globe your potential workplace. And that, my aspiring nomadic compatriot, is the very essence of modern empowerment. Welcome to the future; it fits neatly into your backpack.

Communication and Productivity

Navigating the waves of digital nomadism isn't just about finding the right beach to work from or the perfect cafe with the fastest Wi-Fi. At its core, it's about mastering two critical aspects of remote work: communication and productivity. These are the sails that will propel your ship through the often-unpredictable waters of working while wandering.

First up, let's talk communication. You're on one continent, your client's on another, and your project manager's somewhere in between. The old nine-to-five chat by the water cooler? Long gone. Now, your communication tools are your lifelines. Whether it's Slack pings, Zoom calls, or Trello boards, these tools connect you to your team, your clients, and your projects. But it's not just about the tools themselves, it's also about how you use them. Effective communication as a digital nomad means being clear, concise, and considerate of time zones when sending off that flurry of messages or setting up meetings. It means understanding the nuances of digital etiquette and embracing the asynchronous dance of today's collaborative ventures.

When it comes to productivity, there's an app for just about everything. A temptation indeed, but the savvy nomad knows that less is often more. It's not about having a dozen apps to manage your to-do list; it's about finding that one app that you'll actually use. It's about creating systems and routines that travel with you. Your productivity strategy might involve waking up at dawn to hammer out a few hours of focused work or breaking up your tasks with short, invigorating breaks - perhaps a quick dip in the ocean or a jaunt around the local market.

There's this magical thing that happens when you hit your stride with communication and productivity – it's like finding your flow state. You're engaged, your work has purpose, and your clients are happy. But getting there requires discipline. It's about setting boundaries, like when to sign off for the day or when not to check emails. Remember, the laptop can close just as much as it can open.

Have you ever been stalled by a spotty internet connection right before a deadline? For digital nomads, solid connectivity is your beacon in the night, guiding you toward productivity shores. Therefore, sure, hunt down that enchanting off-the-beaten-path destination, but also be sure you won't be left in digital darkness when you need to shine professionally.

Collaborating across different time zones can feel like trying to sync up with a world that's forever spinning – because, well, it is. Here's a pro tip: get comfortable with tools that help you visualize your team's schedules. When you can clearly see the overlap between your day and theirs, you can pinpoint the perfect moment for real-time collaboration. And for everything else, there's trusty old email, patiently waiting in your inbox.

We can't ignore the reality – staying productive is a challenge when the world's novelties beckon you to play. That's where setting expectations comes into play. Inform your clients and colleagues about your working hours and stick to them. They'll appreciate the transparency, and you'll forge trust along the way. Blending freedom with responsibility is the spell that binds the enchantment of digital nomadism.

Let's dive into tools of the trade for productivity. Think of project management platforms as your virtual office space. They are your desks, your sticky notes, and your calendars all rolled into one. Use them to keep track of assignments, deadlines, and to dos. A clear visual of your productivity landscape helps to maintain focus—no matter if the backdrop is a bustling city or serene mountains.

Your digital toolkit should also include a healthy mix of concentration enhancers. I'm talking about noise-cancelling headphones to drown out the cafe clamor, focus apps to blacklist addictive websites during work hours, and perhaps a soothing playlist of ambient sounds to set the work mood just right.

Now, there's a delicate balance between staying connected and becoming consumed by notifications. To walk this tightrope, become a master of notifications. Customize them, so you only get interrupted for the truly important things. For everything else, carve out specific times to check in – it keeps the chaos at bay and your mind clear.

Continuing the journey, remember that being a digital nomad is as much about flexibility as it is about reliability. Thus, harness the power of cloud storage. Why? Because nothing says 'I've got this' like pulling up a document on any device, anytime, anywhere – all while maintaining the sacred integrity of your workflow.

Communication isn't just about talking shop. Building relationships with your global colleagues and clients goes a long way. Take time for virtual coffee chats or a friendly check-in. After all, nomadism is as much about connecting with others as it is about exploring new territories.

Lastly, integrate wellness apps into your routine. Mental clarity fuels productivity, and whether it's meditation apps to start your day with a clear head, exercise to keep the blood flowing, or nutrition trackers to ensure you're fueling your body right - each plays a crucial role. Like a well-tuned engine in a ship, your well-being drives you forward.

Productivity as a digital nomad isn't a destination; it's a manner of travelling. You'll continuously adapt to new environments, tools, and workflows. The key lies in being agile, patient, and persistent. By doing so, you'll not only reach your professional destinations but also savor the remarkable voyage along the way.

Embracing communication and productivity as pillars of your nomadic lifestyle doesn't just lead to success in work; it elevates the entire experience of being a digital nomad. It turns challenges into opportunities and distant horizons into home. So gear up with the right tools, cultivate robust habits, and watch as the world becomes your office – an office with an ever-changing, brilliant view.

Chapter 4:
Planning Your Nomadic Journey

Imagine standing at the cusp of liberating change—the map unfurls, the screen glows, and a tapestry of connections pulls taut across the globe. You're ready to join the evolution, to take work from cubicles to the rhythm of new cities and cafés. Yet, there's a knack to weaving these aspirations together without fraying the edges. It's about plotting a course that harmonizes with the rhythms of remote life, where personal fulfillment dances with professional commitment. So let's sketch out your transition plan; consider it the compass rose of your future. We won't just scribble lines from point A to B, but rather, draw a constellation that guides you through balancing wanderlust with deadlines, tethering dreams to reality. Each personal and professional goal is etched with intention, bolstered by a steady pace that ensures sustainability over fleeting whims. This is the blueprint of a masterful journey, not just a leap into the unknown. It's your narrative to craft, with every chapter unfolding under different skylines, a story anchored by foresight and strategy, setting the stage for a life that isn't pinned down, but rather, magnificently unbound.

Setting Goals and Expectations

Embarking on your nomadic adventure without a clear map is like setting sail without a compass—thrilling, sure, but a guaranteed ticket to getting lost at sea. As you shed the cocoon of traditional office life, it's crucial to chart out your destinations, both geographically and professionally. We're not just talking pinning locations on a map here; setting tangible goals and realistic expectations is the cornerstone of sustainable digital nomadism. Think of it as laying the groundwork for a skyscraper. The lofty heights you aim to reach with your career and personal growth need to be backed by a sturdy foundation—your well-thought-out aspirations. You'll weave a tightrope between the thrills of travel and the discipline of work, each step measured, each milestone a testament to your foresight. This dance of desire and duty isn't just sublime; it's essential. You're scripting the adventure of a lifetime, so let's get the plotline poised for greatness, shall we?

Personal and Professional Aims Diving into the heart of personal and professional goals, vision sharpens and purpose intensifies. Every decision, every waypoint on the nomadic trail, matters significantly. First off, establishing aims is not just about making ends meet while soaking up sunsets on foreign horizons. It's about curating a life that balances the thirst for exploration with a sustainable career—one that doesn't just survive but thrives in the fluidity of a nomadic lifestyle.

Charting these aims requires a swivel from your conventional perspective on success. It's about recognizing the freedom to choose work that fulfills you while also giving you the flexibility to immerse in the cultures of the world. Think longevity; think passion projects. What professional trajectory appeals to you when the scenery changes with the whim of your heart?

Personally, your aims may orbit around experiencing life to the fullest. Perhaps it's learning new languages, summiting peaks, or mastering the art of Thai cooking. It's important to remember that these personal quests are not distractions—they're vital to the richness of your nomadic experience and are often intertwined with professional growth.

Professionally, aims can vary from seeking remote work that aligns with your skills, branching into freelancing, or launching a location-independent business. Some pursue the dream of passive income streams; others flourish in interactive roles that span time zones and tap into global markets.

While setting these aims, it's vital to distinguish between aspirations that push you and fantasies that distract you. Evaluate what skills you possess and those you need to acquire, understanding that constant learning is the lifeblood of a successful digital nomad.

Delineating these aims should be an exercise in honesty. It's essential to gauge your risk tolerance and align your lifestyle with it. Can you stomach the ebb and flow of freelance work, or would a stable remote role with a firm foundation better suit your temperament?

Networking becomes an extension of both personal and professional targets. Building a diverse global network can transform opportunities, manifesting in unexpected collaborations and cultural exchanges that enrich both your career and life.

For many, the overarching professional aim is autonomy. This might manifest in the form of consultative work, remote gigs with multiple clients, or digital entrepreneurship. The key is to carve out a professional niche that you can carry with you, irrespective of the pin on the map.

Professionals transitioning to digital nomadism often share a core aim: to rewrite the script of what a successful career looks like. This could mean prioritizing work-life balance, or it could involve setting benchmarks for career progression that aren't necessarily tied to a corporate ladder.

The personal aim of connection often accompanies the nomadic journey. Whether it's connecting with nature, with other cultures, or with like-minded individuals, your path should open doors to form meaningful relationships that transcend geographical boundaries.

Aims evolve, and that's not just expected but encouraged. As a digital nomad, the fluidity and unpredictability of your environment will often highlight new passions and skills, urging a recalibration of your goals. It's a process, an ever-unfolding map with multiple routes to explore.

Balancing these aims also requires the right toolkit—digitally and personally. Mastering technologies that facilitate remote work is one slice of the pie; the other slice is nurturing the soft skills, like adaptability and resilience, that you can't plug into a USB port.

Clarity in your personal and professional aims is akin to a compass in the hands of a seasoned explorer. It guides when the path blurs amidst crossroads or when storms rage. With clear aims, even wandering feels purposeful, and each step accrues value in the grand ledger of life.

Don't forget the joy that comes with the pursuit of these aims. There is splendor in the chase, the rough-hewn path that leads to peaks where personal satisfaction merges with professional fulfillment. It's a journey, after all, that molds your story—one that you'll narrate with pride amid the backdrop of your next adventure.

Finally, ensure that your aims are aligned with the core reason behind your choice to become a digital nomad. By harmonizing personal desires with professional ambition, the nomadic life can shape not just the way you work, but more profoundly, the person you become. So embrace this creative challenge to design a life that doesn't just accommodate wanderlust but evolves through it—in your work, in your growth, and in the legacy you choose to leave behind.

Balancing Travel with Work emerges as the crux of sustaining your nomadic lifestyle over time. It's a dance of discipline and desire, strategy and spontaneity. Imagine this: You're basking in the glow of a Bali sunset—but your Slack notifications are glowing too, signaling that clients from different time zones need your attention. Here, in this idyllic yet demanding scenario, is where your prowess in juggling the call of adventure with professional obligations will truly shine.

Ever noticed how the best jugglers make it look effortless? That's because they follow a rhythm, an almost musical timing to their throws and catches. Similarly, blending travel and work demands a rhythmic approach—one that involves punctuating periods of deep work with intervals of exhilarating travel. And just like any skill, this requires practice. Setting clear boundaries between work time and exploration time is essential. It all starts with mastering the art of saying 'no.' An invitation for a spontaneous island hop sounds amazing, but if a deadline looms, it's important to prioritize and decline gracefully.

Technology is both a vessel and an anchor. It enables your nomadic life, but without discipline, it can chain you down. Leverage those tech tools, but don't let them rule you. Use communication apps to manage expectations with colleagues, and project management software to stay ahead of your responsibilities. Adopt the mindset of working smarter, not harder. Automating routine tasks frees up more time to relish in the wonders of your current destination.

Time management transforms from a mundane concept to your everyday accomplice. Knowing your peak productive hours and aligning them with work can carve out swathes of time for exploration. Are you a morning person? Knock out that project at dawn and have the rest of the day to yourself. Maybe you thrive when the world's asleep? Then schedule your sights to see during daylight, and burn the midnight oil when it's time to get down to business.

Every digital nomad knows the gravity of reliable internet access. Don't let connectivity issues strand you in a work void. Research the digital infrastructure of your next stop and always have a backup plan—like a trusty hotspot device. Still, sometimes the universe throws you a curveball, and the Wi-Fi gods frown upon you. Adaptability is your best friend in these moments, finding alternative ways to be productive until you can sail back into the online world.

While the globe is your office, the world isn't on your schedule. Time zones can be tricksters but manage them right, and they become advantageous. They can extend your workday or cut it short. Aligning your schedule with your clients or team may mean unconventional hours, yet it opens up swathes of daytime for you to enjoy your travels. The key is in synchronizing the rhythm of your work with the heartbeat of the world.

Self-care shouldn't be a casualty in the balancing act. Working remotely can blur the lines between personal and professional life. Integrate rituals that signal the beginning and end of your workday, even when swapping out office walls for beachfront vistas. A morning run or an evening meditation can serve as perfect bookmarks to your work chapters, ensuring you're recharged and present for both job and joy.

Maintaining productivity while globetrotting hinges not just on your habits but also on the company you keep. Surrounding yourself with like-minded individuals, whether through co-working spaces or digital nomad communities, instills a sense of shared motivation. When you see others balancing their responsibilities with adventures of their own, it fosters a community of accountability and support.

Then, there's the art of strategic packing—minimalism isn't just a lifestyle, it's a necessity. The gear you carry should serve multiple purposes, favoring versatility over volume. Your laptop is your livelihood; your smartphone, a multifunctional device. From power banks to cloud storage, choose tools that multiply your efficiency while minimizing your baggage.

Navigating the fiscal aspects also plays a significant role in the balancing act. Budgeting becomes an essential skill, as unforeseen travel expenses can crop up. Diversify your income streams if possible, and always have a financial cushion to fall back on in case of emergencies. With smart financial planning, the world is not just a playground, but a place of sustainable living.

There's also the matter of honing your craft continuously. The landscape of remote work is ever-shifting, and so must be your skills and knowledge. Whether it's mastering a new project management tool or learning a language to enhance your travel experiences, invest in expanding your abilities. Personal growth feeds professional success and vice versa.

Let's not forget that as a digital nomad, your work isn't confined to the backlog of tasks waiting on your to-do list. It's about creating, connecting, and contributing to the projects that ignite your passion. When your work aligns with your values and aspirations, it doesn't feel like a ball and chain, even when sipping a cappuccino in a charming European cafe. It feels like an expression of your journey, an integral part of the exploration itself.

Lastly, embrace the fluidity of your routine. While structure is important, the nomadic lifestyle is inherently unpredictable. The ability to pivot with circumstances, to transition smoothly from work mode to travel mode, is what turns challenges into opportunities for growth and enjoyment.

The dynamic of balancing travel with work isn't just about logistics; it builds character. As you navigate through time zones, manage deadlines against backdrops of unexplored cities, you're not just working and traveling—you're evolving. You're becoming more adaptable, resilient, and enriched by every contrasting experience.

And so, in mastering this balance, you find the ultimate expression of freedom. Yes, it's peppered with moments of stress and deadlines, but also filled with the laughter of newfound friends, vistas that steal your breath away, and the sweet satisfaction of living on your own terms. As you step onto the road less traveled, remember that balance isn't just about standing still—it's about moving gracefully through the world, with your work and wanderlust in perfect harmony.

Creating a Sustainable Transition Plan

Embarking on your nomadic journey can spark an exhilarating whirlwind of freedom and adventure, but hold on a sec—it's crucial to channel that excitement into creating a sustainable transition plan. This is the backbone of a successful shift into digital nomadism where your lifestyle becomes synergistic with your career aspirations, and where daydreams morph seamlessly into your everyday reality.

First, take a deep breath and zoom in on the big picture. What does sustainability mean to you in the context of digital nomadism? It's about ensuring that your wanderlust doesn't overshadow the practical aspects of work and living. It means setting up systems and habits that support a long-term commitment to this lifestyle, not just a fleeting escape.

Start by scratching out a timeline. Envision the checkpoints along your transition—like securing remote work, going minimalist with your possessions, or even completing a trial run in a nearby town. These milestones will guide your journey and make sure you're progressing towards your goals without feeling overwhelmed.

Next, let's get down to the nitty-gritty of financial health. It's seductive to think that living the dream doesn't need a budget, but money is the invisible thread that stitches the fabric of nomadism together. Calculated budgeting and savings plans will give you a safety net for when times get tough and allow you to revel in your experiences without the sword of financial woes dangling overhead. Think long-term and make financial stability a cornerstone of your plan.

Equally important is aligning your career path with the remote work scene. If your current job can't be done remotely, it's time to pivot. This may mean upskilling, retraining, or even taking a sideways step career-wise to fit into the digital nomad mold. Keep learning and stay flexible; the remote work landscape is forever in flux.

When you think sustainability, don't forget about personal resilience. Transitioning to a life on the road can be as taxing mentally and emotionally as it is exciting. Cultivating a self-care routine that travels with you is vital. Decoding different time zones while keeping up with professional demands requires mental agility and hardcore organization—equip yourself with tools and habits that support both.

Now, about where you'll plant your feet—or laptop, more fittingly. Geographical strategy is paramount. Research destinations with a sharp eye on cost of living, internet reliability, community vibe, and your own bucket-list. Scrutinize whether you prefer chasing endless summer or if you thrive in changing seasons. Your locations can energize you or exhaust you, so choose wisely.

Connectivity isn't just about internet speeds, though. Building and maintaining a robust online network is also part of a sustainable plan. Loneliness can be a real challenge on the road, but a virtual water cooler of contemporaries is just a videocall away. Engage with digital nomad forums and social media groups; these can be your lifeline for support, inspiration, and even friendship.

Of course, no plan is fail-proof. Hiccups and unexpected turns are part of the adventure. Flexibility is your best friend here. It allows you to navigate through choppy waters with ease and resilience. When things don't go as planned, adaptability will be the skill that keeps you afloat and thriving.

A healthy dose of pragmatism won't go amiss either. Prepare for those less-than-glamorous aspects of nomadism—the visa hurdles, healthcare navigation, and time zone tangles. Address these head-on in your plan with thorough research and contingency strategies. This groundwork will diminish stress and make problem-solving on the go a much smoother process.

And what about those who share your journey? If you're not going solo, incorporating partners, family, or even pets into your nomadic lifestyle requires its own detailed planning. Keep open lines of communication about expectations and responsibilities to ensure that everyone's on the same chapter, if not the same page.

Let's not ignore the physical health department either. Regular exercise and healthy eating habits can be challenging to maintain when you're frequently changing locations. Yet, they're essential to your overall well-being. Think about how you can integrate fitness and nutrition into your routine in a way that's adaptable to various environments.

Finally, to forge sustainability, anchor back to your 'why.' Remind yourself frequently of the reasons you're choosing this lifestyle. Whether it's the thirst for adventure, the desire for flexibility, or the drive to break out of the 9-5 mold, your 'why' will keep you grounded and motivated when the going gets tough.

Consider your transition plan as a living document. It's not set in stone. It evolves as you do. Regularly revisiting and tweaking your plan will help you maintain alignment with your personal and professional growth. This might mean adjusting financial goals or re-evaluating destinations. Keep it alive, keep it kicking.

In conclusion, a robust, flexible transition plan carves out the path for a sustainable nomadic lifestyle. It's the safety harness that frees you to soar. With careful preparation, an agile mindset, and relentless pursuit of balance, your nomadic journey won't just be a fleeting fantasy—it'll be a sustainable, fulfilling way of life. Embrace the adventure, but ground it in reality. With this plan, you're not just drifting—you're steering your ship towards the horizon of your most vibrant dreams.

Chapter 5:
Building a Remote Career

In the refreshing aftermath of mapping out the contours of your transition plan, we pivot to the thrilling quest that is building a remote career. Navigating this landscape is akin to crafting art; it's an intricate dance of aligning innate abilities with the wealth of remote possibilities flourishing in today's cloud-powered marketplace. This chapter isn't just about the scramble to clinch gigs or the hollow hunt for a paycheck; it delves into a thoughtful alignment of your skill set with the booming demand for digital expertise. It's you tapping into continuous learning, honing skills specific to a virtual vocation that plays to your strengths and passions. Imagine for a moment the wide avenues of networking and personal branding. They're more than buzzwords; they're your tools to carve out a reputation in the digital coliseum, connecting you with allies and opportunities that resonate with your newfound freedom. So, let the spark of aspiration ignite your journey – for it's not just a remote career you're building, but a life rich with autonomy and adventure.

Aligning Skills with Remote Opportunities

Imagine harnessing your unique talents and steering them towards a vast sea of remote opportunities that not only demand them but also resonate with your passion for adventure. That's where the rubber meets the road in this chapter. We dive into the art of matching your skill set with remote possibilities that let you thrive professionally while enriching your nomadic lifestyle. Think about it: your skills are like keys, and there's a lock out there in the digital world just waiting to be opened by you. Whether you're a coding wizard, a design maven, or a marketing guru, there's a platform out there that needs what you've got. But here's the kicker—you'll likely want to amp up your skills or even pick up some new ones along the way, because staying one step ahead is part of the game. So as we pivot towards untapped digital domains, let's keep our eyes peeled and our skill sets sharp, ready to tap into a world where work comes with a backdrop of ever-shifting horizons.

Identifying High-Demand Digital Roles So, you've got the spirit of a digital nomad humming through your veins. You're ready to unshackle from the traditional office, merge daily grind with global exploration, and redefine what 'work' means. But where do you fit into this vast digital landscape? That's where pinpointing high-demand digital roles comes into play. It's not just about finding a job, it's about discovering your niche in a market that's hungry for your skills.

First, let's talk tech. As much as we'd like to believe we can wing it, at the end of the day, the tech industry is the backbone of digital nomadism. Software development, cybersecurity, and data science aren't just buzzwords; they're sectors desperately seeking talent. Learning a coding language or two can open doors to freelance gigs, remote contracts, and even full-time positions with companies that don't care where your desk is located, as long as you deliver.

However, not every digital nomad has to speak in JavaScript or Python. There's incredible demand for digital marketing mavens – SEO specialists, content creators, social media managers – those who can navigate the ever-changing landscape of the web to make brands shine. Digital marketers hold the keys to a kingdom where engagement means everything.

But it's not just about the deep dive into algorithms; it's also about aesthetics. Graphic designers and UX/UI experts are in high demand. In a world increasingly driven by visual impact, having a keen eye for design can secure you a spot in the remote workforce. Delivering eye-catching websites, intuitive app interfaces, and engaging visual content can make you an indispensable part of any team.

Sure, we're in the golden age of tech, but let's not overlook writers and editors – the storytellers of the digital age. Quality content is a cornerstone of the online experience, and businesses need talented wordsmiths to articulate their narratives and communicate with audiences. Whether you're crafting blog posts, eBooks, or web copy, your ability to wield words can solidify your role in the remote realm.

And, of course, there's the realm of project management. Those who can lead teams, manage workflows, and keep projects on task and under budget, regardless of timezone differences. If you've got a knack for orchestration, from Asana to Zoom meetings, you're more valuable than you might think.

Now, let's weave another thread into our digital tapestry – customer service. Believe it or no, the personal touch hasn't been lost in the digital age. Customer service and technical support specialists who can solve problems and soothe frustrations with a smile (even through a screen) are worth their weight in bitcoin.

Meanwhile, in the cavernous world of data, analysts and specialists who can turn numbers into narratives find themselves in a favorable position. Companies are swimming in data but struggling for insights. If you can use analytical tools to extract the stories hidden in spreadsheets, you'll never be short on opportunities.

Speaking of tools, let's not forget the digital nomad's bread and butter – remote collaboration and virtual assistance services. Resourceful individuals who can provide impeccable administrative support from afar can build an entire career on the premise of virtual assistance.

And then there are the educators and trainers. The explosion of e-learning platforms has created a thriving space for online educators. If you can teach a language, share expertise in a professional skill, or guide someone through a yoga sequence from the other side of the planet, you're in business.

How about the art of sales? Yes, even here, in the digital domain, there's a sharp need for those who can close deals, nurture leads, and drive revenue – all while maintaining the nomad's transient lifestyle. Top-notch sales professionals who can forge strong relationships despite the lack of a handshake are finding success in the virtual marketplace.

It's clear, right? The digital economy isn't slowing down, and the opportunities for remote work are expanding in all directions. But identifying high-demand roles is only the first step. The challenge lies in matching your passions and skills to these roles. The future of work isn't just about adapting; it's about thriving in fluidity, shimmering with skills that transcend borders.

Remember, your worth doesn't diminish with the miles you travel – it amplifies. As you hustle across time zones and cultures, as you connect with clients and colleagues you've never met in person, you're proving that today's currency is talent, adaptability, and the ability to deliver, no matter where on this blue and green globe you find Wi-Fi.

In your journey, keep a pulse on the market – subscribe to newsletters, join digital nomad hubs online, and stay active in communities. This isn't just networking; it's vital reconnaissance. It ensures that you're not just riding the digital wave but cutting through its crest, board steady, eyes on the horizon.

As you carve your path, don't be afraid to remold your role. You may start as a content writer and evolve into a content strategist, or leap from graphic design into brand consultancy. Flexibility isn't just a perk of being a digital nomad; it's a requirement for staying relevant.

So, who are you in this digital equation? What's the role that not only needs you but fulfills you? Take a breath, define your skill set, glance at the market, and dive in. The beauty of this digital nomadic life is in its boundless potential, sketched against a backdrop of shifting demands and endless skies. Find your spot, tighten your grip, and let's make waves.

Continuous Learning & Skill Development As you etch your mark in the virtual sands, it's essential to keep your skills as sharp as ever. In the realm of digital nomadism, the landscape shifts just as frequently as the locales in your Instagram stories. Continuous learning isn't merely an option; it's the jet fuel for your remote career trajectory.

The necessity for skill development isn't a new concept, but within the perimeters of the digital nomad lifestyle, it takes on a heightened significance. Your ability to adapt and grow determines not only your competitiveness but also your potential for meaningful work-life integration. In this life, laced with freedom and flexibility, becoming a lifelong learner isn't a buzzword—it's your modus operandi.

To thrive, it's critical to identify your knowledge gaps and seek resources to bridge them. Online courses, webinars, and workshops are at your fingertips, giving you the education of a classroom without the confined walls. Digital platforms like MOOCs (Massive Open Online Courses) open doors that were once exclusive to those who could afford the time and expense of traditional education.

Focus on skills that are in high demand in the remote marketplace. Whether it's coding, graphic design, digital marketing, or anything in between, proficiency in these areas could be your ticket to uncharted territories—both career-wise and in your explorations. And don't forget the often underestimated softer skills like communication, time management, and critical thinking, which shine brightly when you work across different time zones and cultures.

As a digital nomad, customization is key. Tailoring your learning path to intertwine with your career objectives helps ensure that every hour spent studying propels you towards your goals. You're not just learning on the fly; you're crafting an educational journey that mirrors the uniqueness of your lifestyle.

Networking too can be a learning experience. Engage with like-minded individuals, mentors, and professionals in your field. Communities, both online and in the co-working spaces you'll frequent, are rich soils for the seeds of knowledge. Never underestimate the power of a conversation—it could lead to a revelation or an opportunity.

Mastery doesn't happen overnight; practice is part of the parcel. Make time to hone your skills through real-world application. Freelance projects, passion pursuits, or even voluntary gigs can serve as practical classrooms where theories are put to the test and skills are refined. It's this hands-on approach that cements knowledge far more effectively than passive absorption.

Don't shy away from the unconventional sources of learning. Podcasts, ebooks, and blogs tailored to digital nomads contain nuggets of wisdom and actionable insights. Surrounding yourself with diverse voices equips you with a versatile toolkit ready to tackle a spectrum of scenarios.

Staying ahead of the curve involves monitoring the trends in remote work and related technologies. As new tools and platforms emerge, earn the ins and outs quickly and become proficient enough to leverage them in your work. Being tech-savvy is no longer optional; it's a core must-have for embracing digital nomadism fully.

Learning isn't limited to pre-defined curricula. Reflect upon your experiences; each new culture and locale offers lessons that transcend conventional wisdom. The success in your next project might just hinge on the adaptability or cultural insight garnered from your last adventure.

Embrace the mentality that every day is a school day. Seek feedback, critique your own work, and continuously iterate on your process. Your growth as a professional mirrors the iterative nature of technology—you both evolve or risk obsolescence.

Keep track of your progress. Documenting your learning journey not only serves as a motivator but also as a portfolio of your ever-expanding capabilities. As you traverse the globe, your documented skills and experiences become your personal brand, speaking volumes to prospective employers and clients.

Lastly, remember that the journey of continuous learning is a personal one. It's about finding the balance that works for you. Some days, it's a deep dive into a complex topic. Other days, it's the subtle learning from new experiences. But every day, no matter how small the step, commit to moving forward, soaking in new knowledge like the sun's rays on a tropical beach.

So chart your course, set sail, and let the winds of knowledge guide you to ports you've yet to imagine. Your career as a digital nomad will thank you for it, as will the countless horizons begging to be discovered through the power of your deepened wisdom and honed skills.

Networking and Branding in the Digital Space

So, you've embraced the digital nomad lifestyle. You've held the globe in your palm, felt that enticing mix of joy and trepidation at the thought of your unfolding journey. Now it's time to talk about carving your niche in the vast digital expanse. Networking and branding - these aren't just buzzwords; they are your bread and butter in the remote wilderness. They are the tether that connects your island to the mainland, your personal trail of breadcrumbs that leads opportunities right to your door.

First things first, let's shatter the myth: networking isn't about exchanging pleasantries and business cards at stiff gatherings anymore. It's about relationships, and thanks to technology's leaps, those connections are just a click away. You might be nestled in a beach bungalow in Bali or sipping espresso in a bustling Roman cafe, but you can reach out to industry leaders, future colleagues, or mentors anytime. Social media platforms, online forums, professional networks like LinkedIn - these are your arenas. Stroll in with confidence, not just a virtual handshake.

Success in the etheric job market doesn't simply hinge on what you know, but who knows you. Remember, visibility is the name of this game. Start a blog, hop onto podcasts, speak at virtual conferences, share your insights on social media. When your voice becomes familiar, your expertise acknowledged, your value well understood - that's when you're more than a name on a screen. You're a voice that matters in your field.

Still, while online networking is integral, don't discount the power of in-person connections. Co-working spaces are fertile ground for serendipitous meetings. The camaraderie of shared experiences can be powerful. Drop in, share your journey, listen to stories, exchange tips. Often, the most fruitful relationships are rooted in real-world interactions.

Building your personal brand in this limitless space is akin to storytelling. What's fascinating about your journey? What unique skills do you inject into your work? Your brand is your story's protagonist – make it compelling. Craft an authentic narrative and resonate with it through all your channels. In the fabric of the digital world, let your brand be the bold, vibrant thread that catches the eye.

Content is your currency. Whether it's writing, graphics, videos, or podcasts, your content should echo your brand's value and mission. It should solve problems, answer questions, and above all, add value. When your content starts conversations, you're on the right path. Engage with your audience, reply to comments, join discussions. And remember – consistency is key. Regular updates keep your audience looking forward to your next post, your next insight, your next innovation. Embrace your unique voice, that's what makes your brand irreplaceable.

What about tying your nomadic nature into your branding? This global perspective you're gaining a broadens your outlook in ways that are highly sought after. Companies treasure worldly, culturally savvy individuals who bring new perspectives to age-old problems. Your travels, the diverse cultures you immerse in, the international networks you build – they are not just life experiences; they're professional assets. Flaunt them.

Take search engine optimization (SEO) seriously. When individuals or companies look for experts in your field, you don't just want to be an option, you aim to be the top choice. Optimize your online content so search engines become your silent promoters. Keywords, hashtags, backlinks – these are the tools that increase your discoverability in the vastness of cyberspace.

Establishing a solid digital footprint, however, isn't a wild dash to the finish line. Yes, be current and quick but don't chase every fleeting trend. What's far more important is aligning your online activities with your long-term vision. When your digital identity echoes your deepest work values and philosophies, it becomes a magnet for companies and clients that share those ideals.

Community building is not just about surrounding yourself with like-minded people. It's about creating a space where your brand can contribute, lead, and inspire. Online groups and forums dedicated to your field or the digital nomad community itself can become your tribe. You encourage, challenge, and support each other. It's symbiotic growth – as you invest in your community, so does it in you.

Let's not forget the power of mentorship. A guiding hand from someone who's already travelled the path can be a beacon in foggy seas. You're not alone in this transition. Seek mentors online, engage with their content, offer your help, and learn from their trials and successes. In this fluid, constantly evolving landscape, wisdom can be your anchor.

Also, be a mentor. Sharing your knowledge doesn't deplete your well; it deepens it. With each gem you give away, you establish yourself as an authority. When potential employers or clients see you're a fountain of knowledge, they're naturally drawn to you.

Privacy and professionalism are your two watchwords in the online branding bazaar. It's easy to get casual when the world's behind a screen, but remember, the internet never forgets. Uphold professionalism in your interactions, respect your privacy, and steer your digital presence with the same care you do your career.

You'll find that your online influence grows hand-in-hand with your network. As you spread your digital tendrils, collaborating with others in your field elevates your status. It's not just about tagging along on someone else's ride. It's about creating value and capitalizing on shared growth opportunities.

In essence, networking and branding in the digital space are about creating ripples. The waves you start can travel far, transcending physical boundaries and bringing the global community to your virtual doorstep. With a harmonious blend of strategic online engagement and organic, real-life connections, your remote career is no longer just a reality – it becomes a beacon for others who dream to tread the same path. These connections you weave not only embolden your journey but become part of the evolving tapestry of digital nomadism itself.

Chapter 6:
Mastering the Logistics of Nomadism

Having built a foundation for your remote career, it's time to delve into the lifeblood of the nomadic lifestyle – its logistics. It's one thing to dream of a life unbound by conventional restraints, but to successfully navigate this path requires a finesse in handling the nuts and bolts, the not-so-glamorous paperwork, and the shrewd financial foresight that keeps everything afloat. Here, we tackle the complexities of zigzagging across borders with ease, ensuring compliancy with diverse international laws, and keeping your finances pristine and your risks covered. Imagine smoothly transitioning from one place to another, not because of luck, but because you've become adept at juggling visas, tax obligations, and insurance intricacies, mastering the tedious, yet vital, elements that uphold the freedom of nomadism. Embrace the meticulous planning and disciplined organization that form the robust framework upon which the spontaneity and vibrancy of your nomadic life depend.

Legalities and Documentation

Imagine yourself with a laptop by the shimmering Aegean Sea or in a quaint café in the narrow alleyways of Prague—dreamy, right? Now, to make that a reality, you can't sidestep the less glamorous side of nomadism: getting your paperwork in check. This is where the rubber meets the road—ensuring your ducks are in a row, legally speaking. You've got to get a handle on the visas that match your wanderlust, figure out what taxes you're liable for when country-hopping, and don't even think about skimping on insurance; health care doesn't care about your nomadic aspirations. Then there's the deal with a permanent address—a virtual mailbox can become your anchor in a fluid world. Every country has its own song and dance when it comes to the law, so you'll need a ballet of documents choreographed perfectly to meet each tune. Think of it as the backstage pass or the VIP ticket to the nomadic show—and you're in the director's chair, orchestrating every move so that when the curtain rises, you're ready for a seamless performance in the art of living and working anywhere on this big, wide stage we call Earth.

Visas, Taxes, and Insurance When embarking on this audacious journey, you'll encounter a significant intersection where international law, finances, and health converge. Understanding the nuances of visas, taxes, and insurance is your golden ticket to sustained nomadic bliss. It's not exactly the stuff of Instagram glam shots, but stick with me—it's the bedrock of your global adventures.

Visas are your entry to the world's stages, yet they can be as intricate as an origami masterpiece. Most countries welcome tourists with open arms, but as soon as you want to work—even remotely—things get muddier. The variety of visas is staggering, from tourist to business, student to residency, and each has a different spiel. Researching and understanding country-specific requirements isn't just smart, it's essential.

Taxes are that lingering 'plus one' you can't seem to shake off at parties. Just because you're sipping coffee in a Parisian café doesn't mean you can forget your obligations back home. Almost every nation wants a slice of your earnings pie, and the rules change depending on where your bank calls home and where you punch in your digital timecard. Double taxation, tax treaties, and foreign earned income exclusions should become part of your vocabulary. Find an international tax consultant to navigate these choppy waters; it's an investment in peace of mind.

Insurance, often the unsung hero, is the lifeline you don't know you need until you do. Picture this: you catch a pesky bug in Thailand or twist an ankle traversing the Inca Trail. Without proper insurance, you're not just in pain; you're in for a financial bruise, too. International health insurance designed for digital nomads is not just a checkbox on a list; it's your guardian in an unpredictable world.

For visas, always check the expiration date, keep tabs on the number of entries allowed, and know the rules of extension. It's not just a stamp in your passport; it's a legal document. Overstaying your welcome can have serious repercussions, anything from fines to bans on future travel. It's not uncommon for countries to change their visa policies, so keep an ear to the ground, especially if you're a long-timer in any given locale.

Some countries are now offering 'digital nomad visas' that allow you to legally work while soaking in the vistas. These are gold dust. They offer the promise of a hassle-free stay, legitimizing your work status. Be sure to read the fine print, as each country shapes its requirements, income thresholds, and terms of stay.

Back to taxes; the physical presence test and the bona fide residence test are key for US citizens to prove they live abroad for tax benefits. But remember, bona fide is more than a stamp—it's about making a life somewhere. And the 330-day rule for the physical presence test isn't about travel shuffling—intention matters. Keep detailed records, and above all, keep it legit.

For insurance, the adage of 'you get what you pay for' couldn't be truer. When choosing a plan, consider coverage for medical evacuation and repatriation, because in the direst circumstances, you want a guarantee of care or to return home. Look for flexibility too—plans that let you add-on cover or adjust as you move are ideal; your life isn't static, and neither should your insurance be.

And let's talk pre-existing conditions—those little historical hiccups can be pesky. Some plans won't touch them with a ten-foot pole. Others embrace them with open arms, usually for a price. It's a delicate dance of risk and reward to find the right coverage that doesn't leave you vulnerable or empty your wallet.

While it's tempting to brush these things under the traveling rug and deal with them 'later', proactive preparation is your passport to success. Use online forums, connect with other nomads, and never be afraid to ask for advice. In the realm of visas, taxes, and insurance, there are no silly questions. In fact, the silly thing would be not to ask.

And let's not forget about tax-friendly countries and territories. Ever wonder why some digital nomads rave about places like Panama, Portugal, or Singapore? Do your homework, and you might find countries that have rolled out the red carpet for entrepreneurs with tax incentives and programs that could greatly benefit your bottom line.

On the insurance end, don't forget to check if your gear is covered. That laptop and camera aren't just tools; they're your livelihood. Specialized gadget insurance can cover theft, damage, and sometimes even tech support when you're in a foreign land and the language barrier feels insurmountable.

As for retirement – yes, I said it, retirement. It might feel like a speck on the horizon, but setting up an international retirement account or understanding how your nomadic years affect your retirement plan back home is crucial. Start early, contribute regularly, and watch as compound interest becomes your globetrotting companion in your golden years.

For those toying with the idea of dual citizenship or second passports, put down roots with care. It's not just about having an escape hatch; it's about belonging, contributing, and understanding the culture and responsibilities that come with that second flag. Citizenship comes with privileges but also duties.

Lastly, let's normalize the paperwork. Just as you wouldn't leave home without your smartphone, make traveling with your legal and financial documents the new norm. Keep digital copies, know where the nearest embassy or consulate is, and treat these documents as bread crumbs leading you back home should you ever need it.

As with any journey worth taking, the one into digital nomadism is paved with administrative tasks that may feel mundane but are, in fact, as pivotal as the destinations you're aiming to explore. Hurdle over the red tape with grace, and you will find a rhythm that allows for the seamless, boundless exploration you seek. Visas, taxes, and insurance are your lifelines—treat them as such, and they will treat you kindly in return.

Establishing a Virtual Base As we dive into the practicalities of your nomadic shift, let's unpack a pivotal part of the logistics: your virtual base. This isn't merely a footnote in your journey; it's the foundation that supports the verve and vibrancy of your traveling lifestyle. A virtual base is not a mere placeholder—it's a nexus of your professional and personal life swirling in the digital realm.

Imagine a place where all your mails are forwarded, where your banking needs are centralized, or where your business registers its address; this place, your virtual base, exists in the cloud, accessible anywhere, without tying you down to a physical location. Importing the concept of a brick-and-mortar base into the virtual world requires you to set up a reliable digital infrastructure encompassing all the necessities that tether you legally and financially to the world, while enabling utter freedom in where you choose to be.

To establish your virtual base, start by settling on a legal domicile—a place where you'll register for tax purposes and obtain important documents. For many nomads, this is their state of last residence or a state with favorable tax laws. Then, ensure you have a reliable mail forwarding service. This provides an anchor for your correspondence, be it personal or professional, safeguarding against the loss of critical documents and establishing a consistent channel for any physical mail that might come your way.

Your virtual base also includes financial elements. Whether it's opening a bank account with robust online services or selecting a credit card that caters to international transactions and offers travel rewards, the fiscal aspects of your virtual base are instrumental. Consider also the marriage of technology and finance; fintech services can simplify money management across borders, making them an invaluable feature of your virtual repertoire.

What about your career's address? If you're an entrepreneur or freelancer, your business needs a registered address. You might not have a permanent office, but virtual office providers furnish you with an address for registration, giving your clients confidence in your professional permanence. And beyond the address, virtual offices often offer additional services like phone answering and access to conference rooms when you need a physical space for meetings.

Let's talk communication. Your virtual base isn't only about receiving but also about reaching out. An essential component is a reliable communication setup—think phone number, VoIP services, and email—that stays constant no matter where you roam. This consistency isn't just about convenience; it builds trust with your clients or employers who can connect with you as if you were in the next room, rather than on another continent.

Data storage and security are a big part of the picture, too. With the right cloud services, your essential documents, work files, and personal media travel with you, secured behind robust encryption. Investing in secure, reputable cloud services means you won't worry about losing important information to a stolen laptop or a crashed hard drive.

Insurance is a crucial piece of the virtual base that can be easy to overlook. As a digital nomad, obtaining proper health, travel, and equipment insurance is non-negotiable. These protect against unforeseen events and provide peace of mind, letting you focus on your work and explorations without the nagging fear of 'what-ifs'. Ensure your policies are international-ready and can be managed online—after all, your life isn't confined to a single geographical spot.

Now, let's not forget privacy. In establishing your virtual base, consider using privacy services that mask your personal information where possible. This is particularly important when registering domains or setting up services that require an address. Utilizing a legal proxy or privacy service keeps your personal information just that—personal—while still meeting the requirements of transparency and accountability.

Transitioning to a nomadic lifestyle also changes your relationship with possessions. A virtual base supports the ethos of living light by digitizing what you can. From important documents to photo albums, make them digital to keep them close without the physical burden. Less stuff translates to more freedom.

While managing your virtual base, keep an eye on compliance. Laws and regulations evolve, and as a digital nomad, staying abreast of international and local laws affecting your income, taxes, and business structure is imperative. Partner with a tax professional who understands the nomadic lifestyle and can provide guidance customized to your situation. Legal tech services can also streamline your compliance needs through automated updates and reminders.

A well-thought-out virtual base will grow with you. It will adapt to your changing needs and locations. Think scalability when you select services—a bank that expands its digital services in lockstep with tech advancements, or a mail service that can handle increased volume as your business grows.

Certainly, this virtual life isn't without its need for real-world touchpoints. It's why you might occasionally require a co-working space for brainstorming sessions or a bout of focused productivity in a structured environment. Your virtual base should encompass this flexibility, allowing you to access such physical resources seamlessly when the need arises.

In summary, your virtual base is a complex, interwoven tapestry of resources, spanning from your legal mailbox to your cloud-based office suite. It supports, sustains, and remains innately flexible, making it the quiet powerhouse behind the explosive freedom of digital nomadism. With intelligent planning and the right tools, your virtual base will not just be established—it will thrive, nurturing your nomadic ambitions and allowing your untethered dreams to flourish. Now, let's craft that base with precision and foresight, ensuring it's a stronghold that sails smoothly with you across the digital seas and shores.

Financial Planning for the Long Haul

So you've got a taste for the nomadic lifestyle, or perhaps you're already knee-deep in the wanderlust-infused waters of digital nomadism. You've launched this lifestyle on a gleaming wave of optimism. But before going any further, it's time to get real about one thing: money. Let's carve a path through the financial undergrowth to ensure your adventure doesn't hit a dead end.

In essence, financial planning as a digital nomad isn't so different from traditional forms – it's about ensuring that you've got the resources to support your choices, both now and in the future. But, there's a twist. Your financial web, woven with threads of currencies from countries you traverse, requires an extra layer of finesse, one that balances spontaneity with security.

Begin by examining your existing savings. It's the springboard that propels you into the nomadic sphere. How deep is the pool you're diving into? A well-planned cushion can soften the impact of unforeseen expenses or income droughts. Think of it as your financial airbag, keeping you safe in the world's unpredictable streets.

Now, let's chat income streams. It's not just about how much you earn, but how consistently you fill your coffers. Diversification is the name of the game here. Contract gigs, passive income sources, investments – they're all pieces of a well-balanced portfolio. Keep them varied to spread risk and avoid relying too heavily on any single source.

Budgeting takes on a nomadic twist in this lifestyle. Costs can wildly fluctuate from one locale to another. A meal in Southeast Asia can cost less than a cup of coffee in Scandinavia. So, hone your budgeting skills to be flexible, and always prepare for regional cost differences. Track your expenses religiously – there's an app for that – or if you're old school, a trusty spreadsheet will do.

On the subject of expenses, let's talk about the big ones. Accommodation and travel can take chunks out of your wallet faster than you can upload a sunset snap to Instagram. Look into longer-term stays to get reduced rates, utilize points and miles for flights, and always be on the lookout for deals. An ounce of research is worth a pound of cash saved.

Taxes are, well, taxing – and they don't disappear once you set off on your voyage. Navigating the tax obligations of your home country and the places you work in can be a labyrinthine task. It's crucial to understand your tax responsibilities and consider enlisting a professional to help, especially if international waters muddy the financial landscape.

Rainy days come in many forms: a broken laptop, an unexpected visa fee, or an emergency trip home. That's where your emergency fund comes in. Tailor it to cover several months of living expenses, keep it liquid, and let it grow with you. The comfort of a financial umbrella lets you dance in the rain with far less worry.

While you're reveling in the globetrotting lifestyle, consider your future self. Retirement planning might be the last thing on your mind as you sip espresso in a Roman piazza, but future you will thank present you for starting early. Explore international retirement accounts, robo-advisors, and self-directed investment options that cross borders as fluidly as you do.

Insurance, while a grudging expenditure, is a hallmark of adulting – and just as essential on the road as it is at home. Health insurance, in particular, should be an unwavering priority. Remember, getting ill without coverage is as enjoyable as a bad Wi-Fi connection. Investigate travel and health policies geared towards nomads; there are more options now than ever before.

Banking without borders – that's a necessity for a digital nomad. Dealing with multiple currencies? Frequent transfers? Seek out financial institutions that serve the globally mobile, with reduced fees for international transactions and currency conversions. Leverage tech tools that make managing finances a breeze while warding off unnecessary charges.

The currency exchange roller coaster can be a profitable ride or a stomach-churning drop – it all depends on timing and strategy. Keep an eye on currency trends, minimize large transactions during unfavorable periods, and consider forward contracts to lock in rates if you've got payments in different currencies. Smart forex management can save you a small fortune.

What happens if you choose to drop anchor somewhere? Buying property can be both an investment and a commitment to a base camp. It's not a decision to be made lightly but consider the benefits of a home you can rent out while you roam. The world of real estate is varied and vast, so research thoroughly to avoid the quicksand of a poor investment.

Finally, it's worth noting that in the nomadic life, social security has a different beat. Traditional 9-to-5 jobs come with certain guarantees, but in the gig and freelance economy, it's often up to you to create that safety net. Consider long-term disability insurance and other ways to protect your income. Because when the music shifts, your dance shouldn't falter.

As you unfurl the map of your digital nomad journey, plot the financial route with as much care as your physical one. The carefree spirit of nomadism is best enjoyed with a solid financial backbone supporting you. Flexibility, adaptability, and a savvy money sense are the currency of this realm, and with these in your pocket, you can navigate the path less traveled with confidence.

Remember that the world is wide, opportunities are plentiful, and the life of a digital nomad is about more than just surviving – it's about thriving. Embrace the financial planning it entails like you do the adventure because, in the end, they're both integral parts of your nomadic tapestry. Be bold, be wise, and let your finances fuel a lifetime of experiences that are richer than any bank account could measure.

Chapter 7:
Overcoming Challenges and Obstacles

Lifting the veil of digital nomadism, we've romanticized the sun-dappled workspaces and the freedom that tags along. However, it ain't all sunsets and smooth sailings; real talk – every nomad will hit a roadblock or two. In this chapter, we're diving headfirst into the nitty-gritty of those trials and tribulations. Let's talk isolation – it's that silent beast that can turn an idyllic beach workspace into a lonely island faster than you can say "Wi-Fi outage." Burnout, its equally devious cousin, loves to creep up on you when you're overloading your plate to prove that you can work from anywhere. But don't sweat it; we've got strategies up our sleeves for safeguarding your mental mojo and fostering connections that'll stand as firm as your passport's stamp collection. As for the wild waves of certainty and adversity, you're about to become a pro at surfing those, too. Uncertainty doesn't have to be a dirty word, not when you've got a compass in your toolkit that points you back to your north star whenever the coordinates of your life seem off balance. By the time you turn the last page of this chapter, you'll be armed to the teeth with the know-how to turn challenges into launchpads, because that's what sets a true digital nomad apart – the art of bouncing back and finding your footing, no matter where on the map you unfold your laptop.

Dealing with Isolation and Burnout

Let's face it, the nomadic lifestyle isn't always sunset selfies and Wi-Fi by the waves; it comes with its own set of tough realizations like grappling with isolation and burnout. When the initial thrill of hopping time zones starts to wear thin and you're wrestling with a project deadline while stranded in a silent Airbnb, that's when the real challenge kicks in. Look, solitude can be a delicious ingredient for self-growth, but too much and you're bingeing on loneliness. Balancing freedom and discipline, digital nomads must recognize the tell-tale signs of burnout before they scorch that vibrant spark of theirs. Commit to routines that anchor your day, dive into local communities or digital forums where kindred spirits roam, and cherish those pauses that breathe life into work marathons. You've chosen a path where you can be alone in a crowd and crowded in your head; finding your equilibrium is key. Remember, it's essential to lean on your internal compass to navigate through this with finesse, taking care to nourish both the explorer in you and the professional clocking in each day.

Strategies for Mental Health and Wellbeing As digital nomads, our lives can be as exhilarating as they are unpredictable. The allure of distant lands and a fluid routine can sometimes obscure the gritty reality that our mental health needs more attention on this untethered journey than it might in a conventional lifestyle. The first strategy is straightforward yet profound: establish a routine. Though it contradicts the nomad's love for flexibility, a daily regimen offers a reassuring structure amidst flux, anchoring you with consistent sleep, work, and relaxation times.

A powerful companion to routine is mindfulness. Engage with your surroundings and current task, and when the mind wanders to worries or a screen, gently lead it back. You can practice this art anywhere – enveloped by the hush of a mountain or in the bustle of a city square. Mindfulness steadies the pulse of nomadic life and revives our wonder in the everyday experiences we're after in the first place.

Nourish the mind with valuable sustenance, like learning. Whether it's a new language relevant to your current locale, a professional skill, or even a cooking technique, learning keeps the brain agile and engaged. This growth mindset bolsters your sense of progress and self-efficacy, which is key to thriving as a digital nomad.

Human connection is a core element of wellbeing often jeopardized by the nomadic lifestyle. Cultivate it deliberately. Co-working spaces are more than just Wi-Fi hubs; they're social lifelines tethering you to a community of like-minded adventurers. Participate actively, and not just with fellow nomads – immerse in the local culture, forge friendships that could even redefine your understanding of home.

You might not have guessed it, but physical health is a cornerstone of mental wellbeing. A body that's cared for paves the way for a clear and present mind. Regular exercise, be it yoga, running, or dance, produces endorphins that combat stress and anxiety, and not to mention, it's a fabulous way to discover the local scenes where you're staying.

In the tapestry of nomadic life, solitude threads its way through the pattern, for better or for worse. Comfortable solitude breeds self-awareness and creativity, but prolonged isolation can lead to loneliness. Leverage technology to keep the touch of your loved ones' lives just a screen away. Sustain relationships through video calls and cherish those bonds as you would the pristine beaches and ancient ruins that embellish your Instagram.

Speaking of technology, set boundaries around screen time. Notifications can fracture your attention like hairline cracks in a windshield. Be the master of your devices, not the other way around.

Designate slots for checking email and social media. When it's time to disconnect, truly disconnect, and let your senses revel in the tactile world.

Stay grounded by reflecting on your purpose, the 'why' behind this escapade into digital nomadism. When the Wi-Fi falters or the loneliness creeps in, revisit this purpose. It will be the ember that re-ignites your passion and determination to navigate the inevitable ebb and flow of this lifestyle.

Relish in self-care. It's not a luxury; it's essential. Take regular stock of your emotional barometer and heed what your mood and energy levels are telling you. If you sense the creeping shadows of burnout, ease off the throttle. There's no shame in taking a day off to recalibrate—after all, the greatest advantage of this life is the ability to set your own pace.

Journaling is a simple yet transformative practice. It is the repository of your experiences, the good and the challenging. Write without censoring, and you may find clarity and solutions emerging naturally onto the page. Sometimes, the act of writing is all that's needed to unload the weight from your shoulders.

The digital nomad's path is often laden with uncertainty, a factor that if not managed, can unravel one's peace of mind. Approach this unpredictability with a toolkit of resilience strategies - identify the aspects you can control, develop contingency plans, and for everything else outside your control, practice the art of acceptance.

Financial stability is essential to mental wellbeing. While embracing the unpredictable, a safety net of saved funds can cushion unexpected blows and alleviate the anxiety that often comes with financial insecurity. Managing your finances with care can offer peace of mind as steady as any desk job once promised.

Finally, do not underestimate the power of saying 'no.' Just because the world is your oyster doesn't mean you need to explore every inch of it immediately. Align your activities with your energy levels and personal goals. The ability to say 'no' is a hallmark of good self-care and ensures your experiences as a nomad are enriching rather than draining.

To wrap it up, remember that your mental health is just as crucial as the adventure itself. Crafting a fulfilling life on the move isn't just about snapping the perfect sunset for your feed or hustling for the next gig; it's about nurturing the spirit that craves this freedom in the first place. A resilient, well-balanced mind is the most reliable compass you'll have as a digital nomad. So, weave these strategies into your journey, and watch how they enrich the tapestry of your nomadic life and wellbeing.

As the sun sets on this chapter and rises on the next, the strategies for nurturing your mental health and wellbeing illuminate the path forward. Embrace them wholeheartedly, for they're the quiet guardians of your nomadic dreams.

Building a Supportive Community Amidst the thrills of exploring exotic locales and the satisfaction of ticking off work tasks with your feet buried in white sands, there's a less-discussed side of digital nomadism: the potential for isolation. As you migrate from one destination to another, the absence of a stationary support system can leave you feeling unmoored. That's why one of the critical pillars in crafting a fulfilling nomadic life is knitting your own global tapestry of support.

Imagine you're settling into your latest temporary base, a bustling hub in Southeast Asia or perhaps a tranquil beach town in Latin America. The scenery shifts, the cultures evolve, but the need for connection remains constant. Diving into the nomadic lifestyle doesn't mean you must become a lone wolf. In fact, it's the pack – your community – that often sustains your spirits and nurtures your growth.

Start by recognizing that community isn't solely about proximity; it's about shared values, interests, and goals. Look for co-working spaces and frequent them. These are the oases for like-minded individuals where ideas flow as freely as the coffee. Introduce yourself at social events, engage in meaningful conversations, swap expertise, and watch your support network grow as organically as conversations do around shared passions.

Don't underestimate the power of online forums and social platforms either. There are countless groups dedicated to the digital nomad lifestyle where you can seek advice, find companionship, and share your successes and challenges. Engagement in these virtual communities bridges the gap between physical locations, ensuring you have a league of supporters accessible with just a few mouse clicks.

Often overlooked but equally important is fostering relationships with the local community. Bonding with residents can enrich your experience profoundly. You're not just a tourist passing by; you're a temporary local aiming to understand and respect their culture. By learning the language, partaking in local festivities, or simply shopping at the same market, you're sowing the seeds of genuine relationships that often bloom into an extended family.

Volunteering can also be an avenue to build connections while giving back. Whether teaching English, helping with community projects, or conservation work, each act of service links you with locals and fellow volunteers, creating a network founded on altruism and shared experiences.

A mentor or accountability partner can provide an anchor amidst the fluidity of your journey. This relationship brings a sense of stability and continuity to your ever-changing backdrop. These connections don't have to be in person; cyberspace allows for distance-defying mentorships. Regular check-ins with mentors or peers can help you keep focused on your goals and serve as a sounding board for your aspirations or apprehensions.

When you travel, so does your community. The people sitting next to you on a bus ride to Angkor Wat or the couple you meet while hiking in the Andes could potentially become part of your tribe. Don't hesitate to strike up conversations. Exchanging contact information today might lead to a collaborative project or a shared journey tomorrow.

Remember, building a community is synonymous with cultivating a garden; it requires patience, nurturing, and regular attention. As you move, your relationships must be maintained. This might mean scheduling regular video calls, sending updates, or planning reunions. The landscape of your community will diversify as you journey, reflecting the rich array of your experiences and travels.

Embrace the power of storytelling. Sharing your adventures and lessons learned on a blog or a podcast can not only build your community but also position you as a thought leader within the digital nomad world. Listen to other's stories too. The shared narrative of nomadic life is both a bonding agent and a learning opportunity.

In moments of loneliness, don't retreat into your shell. Reach out. Talk to a familiar face from home or to a new friend from your travels. Human connection is not just comforting but essential for mental well-being. Keeping this lifeline active is a preventative measure against the echo chamber of your own thoughts.

Speaking of mental well-being, be proactive about joining or forming mastermind groups and support circles. These small, focused groups can provide both personal and professional support, acting as critical sounding boards for life's complexities and crossroads.

As a digital nomad, you have a unique opportunity to be part of multiple communities – each with its own culture, values, and insights. You're not just building one supportive community; you're weaving a mosaic of interconnected networks that span the globe.

The community you build as a digital nomad can be your pillar in uncertain times. In this ecosystem, you can find potential business partners, lifelong friends, or simply the camaraderie necessary to thrive. It's about understanding that while your office might be virtual and your address ever-changing, your connections are as real and meaningful as any traditional setup.

So, as you pen the next chapter of your nomad diary, keep the doors to your community wide open. An inclusive, supportive network is more than a safety net; it's a trellis on which the vine of your nomadic life can flourish. Craft it with care, nurture it with attention, and watch as it transforms the odyssey of solo travel into a symphony of shared human experience.

Yes, you might have embarked on this path in search of freedom or adventure, but you'll soon discover that interdependence isn't antithetical to independence. On the contrary, in the grand tapestry of digital nomadism, it's the connections you weave along the way that add the most vibrant colors to your journey.

Navigating Uncertainty and Adversity

The life of a digital nomad is sprinkled with excitement and brimming with the allure of freedom. Yet, we'd be glossing over the whole picture if we didn't acknowledge the winds of uncertainty and storms of adversity that are a part of this adventure. It's about more than just dealing with a shaky Wi-Fi connection or finding the best latte in a new city. It's about handling the unpredictable nature of remote work and the ups and downs of leading a nomadic lifestyle.

Uncertainty hangs in the air like fog. Where will your next gig come from? How will you adjust to a sudden change in visa regulations? These are valid yet often daunting questions. The key is not just to survive these setbacks but to turn them into stepping stones. It's like surfing; you've got to ride the waves, not fight them.

The first step is to develop a resilient mindset. Resilience doesn't mean that you won't experience difficulty or distress. It means experiencing those things and still holding true to your nomadic path. Embrace flexibility as your mantra. When one opportunity fades away, pivot your direction and look for another. You'll find that there's always another way, another path, if only you're willing to take it.

Financial uncertainty can be a particularly difficult beast to tame. One day, your PayPal is flush with funds; the next, you're eating instant noodles more often than you'd like to admit. That's where the power of budgeting and an emergency fund comes into play. Treat your finances like you're planning for a siege - stockpile what you can, when you can. When the storms hit, you'll be grateful for the fortress you've built.

Now, let's talk about the random mishaps that can come out of nowhere. Missed flights, lost laptops, sudden illness - these are the travel trials that test your mettle. Adaptability becomes your greatest ally here. Learn to problem-solve on the fly, to assess your options rapidly, and always, always have a backup plan. Remember, every setback is a lesson in disguise, shaping you into a more adept nomad.

Adversity isn't just about external factors, either. It can be internal, too. There will be days when motivation runs dry, when loneliness creeps in as you watch another sunset alone. Strategies for well-being and mental health aren't just nice to have; they're essential. Cultivate a routine that includes self-care, whether that's journaling, yoga, or video-calling friends and family. Your mental and emotional health is the bedrock upon which your nomadic life is built.

Building a supportive community is another lighthouse in the fog of uncertainty. Connect with fellow digital nomads, whether online or in-person at coworking spaces. Share your stories and listen to theirs. These connections can lead to collaborations, opportunities, and a shared sense of understanding that's incredibly comforting on those tough days.

Furthermore, don't underestimate the importance of continuous learning. The digital landscape is ever-evolving, so stay on your toes. Embrace the challenges as chances to grow. Today's obstacle can sharpen your skills for tomorrow's opportunities. Leverage online courses, webinars, and mentorships to enhance your professional arsenal.

Remember, the nature of adversity is often transient. That difficult client, the project that flopped, even moments of self-doubt, they pass with time. What remains are the lessons learned and the resilience forged through the fire of experience. Reflect on these experiences; document them not just for memory's sake, but as signposts for others who will follow in your footsteps.

Insurance, both health and property, is one trick savvy nomads use to mitigate some of the uncertainties of their lifestyle. Yes, it's an added expense, but it's also peace of mind. Whether you're laid up with a fever in Bangkok or facing a broken camera in Barcelona, you're covered.

And then there's the gift of saying "yes" - to opportunities, connections, and experiences that fall outside your comfort zone. Uncertainty breeds possibility, and possibility is the playground of the creative, the brave, the nomads of the world. Say yes more often than you say no, and watch doors open in places you never expected.

Let's not forget the role of intuition. Call it gut feeling, if you will. In a lifestyle that's less structured by default, trusting your instincts is vital. Sometimes, navigating uncertainty means listening to that inner voice telling you to take a leap or to tread cautiously.

While you're blurring the lines on a world map with your travels, remember to leave breadcrumbs for your future self. Document your contacts, keep a record of the jobs you've had, and the experiences you've gained. These notes might just be the map you need when traversing through the fog of uncertainty.

Finally, celebrate every victory, no matter how small. Completed a project on time? Toast to that. Overcame a bout of loneliness? Give yourself a pat on the back. These celebrations are affirmations that you're moving forward, that you're not just surviving the nomadic life – you're thriving in it.

In the tapestry of digital nomadism, the threads of uncertainty and adversity are interwoven with those of opportunity and growth. Learn to view challenges as mechanisms for personal and professional development. Your ability to navigate them doesn't just determine the quality of your nomadic experience; it shapes the essence of who you are as a person and a professional. So go ahead, embrace the journey – every rock-strewn path and sunlit vista. The world is waiting for you to leave your mark.

Chapter 8:
Cultivating a Global Mindset

As we embark on this chapter, let's weave into the rich tapestry of digital nomadism with a crucial thread—cultivating a global mindset. This isn't just about adapting to different time zones or finding the best local coffee spots. We're talking about a comprehensive shift in perspective that allows you to thrive in the kaleidoscope of global cultures. Embracing diversity isn't mere politeness; it's a strategic tool that arms you with empathy, insight, and adaptability. Imagine the taste of Pad Thai in Bangkok informing your palate for better culinary choices, or the meticulous German approach to time influencing your workflow efficiency. A global mindset means leveraging cultural differences to elevate your personal and professional self, while always navigating with respect and curiosity. It's about learning to ride waves of change, with each crest and trough reinforcing your buoyancy and resilience as an international player in this ever-connected world.

Embracing Cultural Diversity

In the grand tapestry of digital nomadism, cultural diversity isn't just a backdrop; it's the vibrant thread that weaves through every encounter, shaping our perspectives and enriching our experiences. When you step out of that familiar cocoon and open your arms to the kaleidoscope of world cultures, you're not just checking off bucket list destinations; you're embarking on a profound journey of personal growth. It's about savoring the spicy tang of street food that sings to your soul in Bangkok, navigating the rhythmic chaos of a bustling Mumbai market, or sharing stories under a starlit sky with new friends in a Moroccan riad. This isn't about merely coexisting with difference; it's about actively engaging with it, letting every new dance, language, and tradition challenge what you thought was set in stone. As nomads, we must be students of the world, shedding biases, embracing empathy, and carrying that spark of human connection that knows no border. Let's not just pass through cultures; let's let them pass through us, leaving us forever changed, intrinsically linked in this shared human experience. Because, in the end, the ability to understand and celebrate our differences is the very essence of a global mindset, and it's this rich palette of perspectives that makes the nomadic lifestyle an endless source of inspiration and growth.

Adapting to Different Environments As we wade deeper into the shimmering waters of digital nomadism, the ability to slip into new environments as effortlessly as changing gears is not just a coveted skill—it's your lifeline. Imagine you're plunged into the bustling streets of Bangkok one week, only to find solitude in a Balinese villa the next. Your workspace oscillates from a Madrid café filled with the resounding clatter of coffee cups to a serene park in Copenhagen. This ever-changing backdrop isn't just scenery, it's the stage upon which you perform the act of work and life.

Adaptability is about more than just finding a new coffee shop; it's a robust cocktail of cultural sensitivity, flexibility, and resourcefulness. Think of it as the Swiss Army knife in your travel pack. Whether it's dodging language barriers like linguistic bullets, or tweaking your sleep pattern to match a new time zone, it's the capability to morph with the surroundings that empowers you to thrive.

Moving from one place to another, you'll notice that productivity doesn't have a one-size-fits-all solution. The distractions in a New York library differ from those in a beachfront in Costa Rica. It's about creating your bubble of concentration, whether that means noise-canceling headphones or finding that golden hour when your energy peaks and the world seems to quiet down just for you.

Picture this: you land in a country where the internet crawls at a snail's pace. Instead of losing your cool because the WiFi won't cooperate, you recalibrate. You plan tasks that require less bandwidth or scout out local co-working spaces that boast high-speed connections. It's this quick-footed dance that sets apart successful nomads from the rest.

You'll also bake into your routine the spice of life—variety. Routine can be treacherous; it can lure you into complacency. By spicing up your surroundings, you challenge yourself to remain agile, keeping your brain nimble and willing to absorb new patterns. This doesn't mean you throw consistency to the wind. Instead, you anchor yourself with a few sacred rituals or routines that travel with you, providing comfort amidst the whirlwind of change.

The art of adaptation also means setting boundaries. Knowing the local customs and how to blend in can make the difference between feeling like an outsider and feeling at home. It's appreciating the need to dress a certain way in conservative countries or understanding workday norms that differ from your own. It's about switching your internal rhythm to match the beat of your new environment. There's a profound elegance in the ebb and flow of this cultural dance.

Develop your sixth sense for functioning in diverse settings. This means honing your situational awareness—being acutely present and observant. It's understanding when it's safe to work from a public park or realizing before it's too late that a storm will soon turn your beach workspace untenable. This type of awareness is priceless and keeps you not just productive, but also safe.

Yet, among all this change, protect your well-being fiercely. Jumping time zones and cultures can disorient even the most savvy of travelers. Recognize the signs of fatigue and give yourself permission to slow down. Adaptation is not about relentless modification—it's also about recognizing when to take a break and recharge. Your health, both mental and physical, is the fuel for your nomadic journey, and it demands respect.

Remember, in each new space lies an opportunity for growth. Locals you meet may teach you an efficiency hack you never knew existed or a lifestyle change that revolutionizes your workflow. Be open to these lessons. Your nomadic path is a journey of continuous learning, with each environment acting as a unique classroom.

Cultivating a global mindset doesn't happen overnight, and adapting to different environments is a centerpiece of this transformation. Observe how people interact, handle business, or even play. These nuances are the brushstrokes of a bigger picture you're painting with each new destination—it's the mosaic of your global experience. These insights allow you to evolve not just into a more effective nomad, but also a more enlightened human being.

The practical side of adapting is just as critical. Master the mundane yet vital aspects of life on the move. From figuring out the best local grocery stores to finding that serene jogging path to clear your mind, these small victories add texture to your nomadic life. Efficiency isn't born in a vacuum; it's shaped by the realities and limitations of the immediate environment.

Equip yourself with tools that foster flexibility. The world may be your office, but without the right tech and apps to support your variable lifestyle, you might find yourself adrift in a sea of unpredictability. Rely on cloud services, portable gadgets, and offline capabilities that secure your ability to work anywhere, anytime, regardless of the whims of your current locale.

And don't forget to infuse your life with the local flavor. Work and culture are not mutually exclusive. Learn the language, taste the local cuisine, and participate in community events. This inclusion not only enriches your experience but also allows you to view your surroundings through a lens of empathy and connection rather than detached observation.

When the world is your office, each pitstop is a chance to redesign your workday. The fluidity of your environment means that stagnation should never be part of the vocabulary. Forging a life on the road requires a cocktail of resilience, improvisation, and eagerness to embrace the novelty that each new dawn brings.

Adapting to different environments is not just a strategy for the digital nomad; it is the very essence of this vibrant lifestyle. With each transition, whether it's a bustling urban center or a tranquil mountain retreat, you're not just finding a new place to work—you're discovering a fresh canvas to shape your life's story, one glorious brushstroke at a time.

The Importance of Cultural Sensitivity As we turn the page on embracing cultural diversity and adapting to various environments, it's crucial to underline the significance of cultural sensitivity, especially when you're navigating the globe with a laptop in tow. Imagine stepping into a new country, armed with skills and an unquenchable thirst for exploration, only to find that the locals are offended by an unknowing breach in their cultural etiquette.

Cultural sensitivity isn't just about avoiding faux pas; it's about deep respect and understanding – learning the subtle dance of social norms and traditions of each place you visit or work from. It might seem daunting at first, but understanding the cultural intricacies can enrich your experience beyond measure and open doors to genuine connections that last a lifetime.

In the realm of digital nomadism, you're not just a tourist passing by; you often merge into local landscapes, work environments, and communities. That means the impact you have is more pronounced, and the importance of being culturally sensitive becomes even more critical. You aren't just representing yourself, but potentially an entire community or the concept of digital nomadism as a whole.

Consider this – as a nomad, your lifestyle might intrigue those you meet, but it also brings a responsibility. Curiosity will often invite questions about where you're from and why you've chosen to work this way. These interactions are a two-way street, exchanges where cultural sensitivity ensures you learn as much about the local customs as they learn about your nomadic way of life.

So, what does being culturally sensitive entail? For one, it's a commitment to ongoing education. Before setting foot in a new destination, take time to research its history, social norms, and etiquette. Look beyond the tourist brochures to understand the cultural do's and don'ts, the religious beliefs, and the political climate. It's this understanding that allows you to thread softly, respecting the cultural tapestry of each unique locale.

Language is another essential aspect of cultural sensitivity. While you might not become fluent in every language, learning a few key phrases can break barriers and warm hearts. It shows an effort to step into another's world, a willingness to communicate even when it's outside your comfort zone. And often, it's that effort that's met with appreciation and openness.

Moreover, cultural sensitivity is about empathy in your everyday interactions. Whether you're engaging with a local vendor, a client from another country, or fellow nomads from diverse backgrounds, the ability to put yourself in someone else's shoes, to understand their perspective, can make all the difference in nurturing a healthy, multicultural workspace and living environment.

Yet, it's about more than just avoiding misunderstandings. Embracing cultural sensitivity means actively participating in local traditions and festivities when appropriate. It means showing interest and respect for local customs and knowing when to observe and when to partake. Through this participation, you're acknowledging the value of local traditions and fostering a greater sense of global community.

Cultural sensitivity also extends into the digital world. With remote work, comes the likelihood of collaborating with teams from all over the globe. Miscommunications can easily arise from cultural misunderstandings or different communication styles. Being culturally sensitive in these scenarios means being mindful of time zones, holiday observances, and the varied approaches to business communications and negotiations across cultures.

Always remember, as a digital nomad, your interactions are not fleeting. The connections you make, business relationships you build, and the friendships you foster all have the potential for long-term impact. Being culturally sensitive can translate into lasting professional connections, repeat business, and collaborative opportunities spanning across continents.

In some ways, being culturally sensitive can also safeguard your well-being. In certain destinations, public behavior that might seem innocuous to you could actually be illegal or gravely offensive. Your awareness and adherence to local laws and customs are not just a sign of respect but also a form of self-protection, ensuring that your nomadic journey isn't derailed by a cultural misunderstanding.

Additionally, as the fabric of our global community evolves, remaining culturally sensitive is not a static task but a dynamic process. What was appropriate a decade ago might not hold today, and what works in one place might be anathema in another. It's this fluidity that keeps the life of a nomad both challenging and exhilarating.

But cultural sensitivity isn't just a self-serving tool; it's an embodiment of compassion and global citizenship. It's understanding that your freedom to explore comes with a duty to honor the cultures that welcome you in. That by being sensitive to the nuances of different cultures, you're contributing to a more understanding, cohesive world – one where the spirit of nomadism thrives on mutual respect.

Embracing cultural sensitivity is a journey in its own right – one that goes hand in hand with the physical travels of a digital nomad. It turns each destination from a mere backdrop for work into a rich, educational canvas, painting your life with experiences that truly resonate. After all, the richness of this lifestyle isn't just found in the places you go, but in the depth of your encounters and the harmony you cultivate with the world.

Learning from International Experiences

Becoming a digital nomad doesn't just mean changing your work environment; it's a passport to a vast library of experiences, stories, and lessons learned from every corner of the globe. As you hop from one time zone to the next, you'll quickly realize that every spot on the map offers a fascinating case study in how to live, work, and flourish.

The beauty of learning from international experiences is that the world itself becomes your most compelling teacher. It's more than scooping up salsa dancing in South America or mastering the art of a Thai curry. It's about absorbing the nuances of communication in each culture, recognizing the ebbs and flows of global markets, and adapting your professional strategies to mesh with a mosaic of business practices and social customs.

Imagine you're in a bustling Southeast Asian city one month, then a quaint European village the next. Both will challenge you in different ways. The key, however, is not just to survive these challenges but to thrive within them. How? By becoming a sponge for local knowledge. The more you learn about how different societies operate, the more you enrich your own toolset. You'll pick up time management skills from Germans, negotiate like a bazaar vendor in Istanbul, and adapt to rapid change as you've seen done in Singapore.

But let's dive deeper. Maybe it's Tuesday, and you're collaborating online with a team that's scattered across four continents. Each member brings their own work ethic, problem-solving approaches, and communication styles. It's a living lab where international experiences teach you how to bridge differences and create synergy. You become adept at leading and following, speaking and listening, teaching and learning. It's a give-and-take dance that can only be learned in the global playground of digital nomadism.

Don't forget that with every stroll down a foreign street, you're also untangling the complex tapestry of local economies. You'll come to see how certain policies impact entrepreneurs in Buenos Aires differently than they might in Berlin. Your understanding of taxation, trading, and market demands won't just be textbook knowledge but grounded in the realities you've seen with your own eyes.

Sure, you'll face language barriers and cultural faux pas, but each misstep is a potential leap forward in personal growth. It's the perfect setting to hone your patience, expand your perspective, and sometimes, to invent entirely new solutions because the conventional ones don't fit. You'll learn to communicate more effectively, not just linguistically but also in conveying your ideas across cultures.

Grasping nuances in body language and etiquette becomes second nature as you interact with locals. What's polite in one place can be rude in another, and digital nomads become connoisseurs of context, tailoring their behavior suitably. This isn't just about good manners—it's a strategic advantage in building networks and negotiating deals.

What's more, every challenge you overcome while navigating these experiences compounds your resilience. When you hit a snag in Morocco, troubleshoot tech issues in Tokyo, or manage deadlines while dealing with Delhi's vibrant chaos, you're not just solving a problem; you're stretching your comfort zone to places you didn't even know existed.

International experiences also embolden you to take calculated risks. You've seen businesses thrive on daring innovation in Silicon Valley and traditional craftsmanship in artisanal Italian workshops. Witnessing this range of success stories expands your mindset to approach risks with a balanced view – calculating the jumps but not hesitating to leap when necessary.

One of the most underestimated aspects of learning from global experiences is self-awareness. As you adapt to different cultures, you can't help but reflect on your own. You'll discover biases you didn't know you had and strengths you hadn't tapped into. This introspection is invaluable in shaping not just your career, but the contours of your very character.

Moreover, think about the networks you build. Each person you meet, whether a fellow nomad, a local entrepreneur, or a chance acquaintance at a hostel, is a node in an interconnected world of ideas and opportunities. The friendships and professional connections you forge can lead you down career paths you never imagined, or offer support during downturns.

In essence, you're not just learning about international markets, languages, and cultural norms; you're experiencing the human condition in all its diversity. It's about celebrating a local festival in Mexico, understanding the significance of silence in a Japanese meeting room, or finding just the right way to express gratitude in Arabic.

And while you're out there gathering stories from the Sahara to the Swiss Alps, remember you're also becoming a story yourself—a protagonist in a tale of someone who dared to step out of comfort zones and chased the sunrise to see what lies beyond. You become a living narrative of adaptability, creativity, and endurance.

As you weave these varied threads into your journey, your expertise will become unique, sought after, and invaluable. That blend of skills is a cocktail not easily replicated, and it's what will set you apart in a digital world hungry for well-rounded, world-aware innovators.

Finally, in this whirlwind of constant change and learning, make sure you're taking a moment to reflect and practice gratitude. Appreciate the diversity that surrounds you and the chance you have to experience this incredible world as your office. The lessons are countless, and they'll come at you fast. Capture them, embrace them, and let them guide you to becoming not just a better professional, but a profoundly richer human being. Welcome to the world, your classroom without borders.

Chapter 9:
The Impact of Digital Nomadism on Society

As the currents of digital nomadism ripple outwards, they touch and transform every shore of society. Imagine a world where rush hours fade and cities breathe anew, as work from anywhere policies empty the offices and populate the parks. This new chapter in human progress reconfigures the urban dynamics, sparking life into co-working spaces and coffee shops while challenging the traditional economic models. As digital nomads, you're not just adventurers charting your own course—you're pioneers of an eco-friendly ethos that challenges us to think globally and tread lightly. Through ethical nomadism, you exemplify global citizenship, celebrating cultural interactions as opportunities to weave a tapestry of understanding and respect. Your lifestyle is less about escaping society and more about reshaping it, offering a blueprint for a world where work adapts to life, rather than the other way around. You're at the vanguard of a societal shift, creating waves that erode old paradigms and sculpt the contours of a future we're all eager to witness.

Remote Work and Urban Dynamics

As we tap into the pulsing vein of digital nomadism, it's impossible to overlook how this lifestyle shakes the very foundation of urban dynamics. Cities, traditionally seen as bastions of economic activity and cultural hubs, are experiencing a metamorphosis sparked by the remote work revolution. Professionals armed with laptops and a thirst for variety are no longer tethered to metropolitan life. Imagine the sheer possibility: a bustling metropolis one month, a seaside town the next, all while your career trajectory soars. This fluidity is morphing the urban landscape, as demand for short-term housing and versatile workspaces surges. Coworking spaces are transforming into hives of innovation, where like-minded digital warriors connect, creating a new urban heartbeat. In this jet-setting era, the concrete jungle's economy diversifies, local businesses thrive with fresh clientele, and the city's environmental footprint is poised for a reckoning. As a prospective digital nomad, you're not just stepping into a lifestyle – you're striding into the forefront of a societal shift that redefines the quintessence of the urban experience.

The Future of Cities and Coworking Spaces Imagine a world where the boundaries of work and lifestyle blur into a magnificent tapestry of experiences, each stitch representing a new opportunity, a diverse interaction, or a personal breakthrough. Cities, traditionally economic powerhouses, are transforming under the nomadic tide, and coworking spaces are the vanguard of this change, becoming beacons for creativity and collaboration.

The essence of urban life is in metamorphosis. No longer are cities merely points on a map where large workforces congregate in tall office buildings. The tapestry of city life is being rewoven with threads of flexibility and innovation, with coworking spaces popping up like wildflowers in an open field. These spaces provide a unique blend of communal and individual work environments that cater to the highly mobile lifestyle of digital nomads.

This new epoch brings with it the reimagining of public spaces and transportation. Parks, libraries, even transit stations, are adapting to cater to remote workers seeking a change of scenery or a temporary respite from their usual haunts. Cities are increasingly recognizing the value of providing free Wi-Fi and comfortable public seating to support this socio-economic shift.

As coworking spaces proliferate, they evolve beyond just shared offices. They embody community centers, incubators for innovation, and staging grounds for globe-spanning projects. Such environments cultivate networks that reach far wider than their physical confines, generating a ripple effect of opportunity and growth across entire urban landscapes.

The influx of nomads into urban settings has a remarkable effect on local economies. Cafés and restaurants buzz with a new clientele; phone repair shops and tech stores see heightened demand; and short-term housing experiences a renaissance, with creative solutions appearing on the scene. These environments are becoming ecosystems that support the nomadic lifestyle in a symbiotic relationship that benefits both the individual and the city.

However, the future of coworking spaces isn't simply about economic symbiosis; it's also about sustainability. The traditional model of 9-to-5 in energy-consuming offices is being upended in favor of shared, efficient spaces that use resources better, stay open longer, and adapt to their occupants' needs in real time.

Looking at the horizon, elements such as smart technology weave into the fabric of coworking locales. Spaces that adjust lighting and heating based on occupancy, use of solar power, rainwater harvesting systems, and even indoor greenery that purifies air – all contribute to an environment that's not just for work, but for living a philosophy of sustainability and consciousness.

Moving forward, as cities contract and expand with the ebb and flow of nomadic populations, policymakers are taking note. Urban planning now accounts for transient populations, weaving coworking spaces into the DNA of city development. Educational initiatives, partnerships with tech firms, and investment in infrastructure support a city's shift from a static to a fluid, dynamic entity.

The coworking spaces of the future are poised to be more than workplaces. Think of them as life hubs – places that offer not just a desk, but wellness centers, daycare facilities, and perhaps even short-term accommodations. They cater to all facets of life, henceforth becoming a cornerstone of the digital nomad's environment.

And it's not just the physical space that's evolving; the services offered by coworking spaces are becoming increasingly sophisticated. From legal and tax advice for the wandering workers to networking events that bring together diverse skill sets and perspectives, the support offered is more akin to that of a community than a mere office provider.

But let's not forget the import of social dynamics. Coworking spaces increasingly facilitate engagement and collaboration. The cultural exchange within these microcosms of society sews the seeds of tolerance, mutual respect, and invaluable learning. These local interactions echo globally as nomads carry insights from one city to the next.

The cities that embrace this evolution stand on the forefront of a new urban revolution. Communities that integrate and cater to digital nomads are likely to see an influx of diverse talent, bringing fresh ideas and innovation and challenging the status quo. They turn into hotspots not only for business but also for cultural and intellectual exchange, fostering an atmosphere of internationalism.

Indeed, the resiliency of coworking spaces in the face of global challenges such as pandemics has shown that adaptability is paramount. With the increase in remote work, the desire for human connection and a structured work environment will drive the metamorphosis of coworking spaces even more. These hubs will likely emerge as a new kind of community center, a focal point for both productivity and social interaction in an increasingly decentralized world.

However, the tale doesn't end in the city centers. As remote work continues to rise, the suburbs and even rural areas will see a shift. Small towns might bloom with coworking spaces, appealing to those nomads seeking solace from urban buzz yet still craving professional community and state-of-the-art amenities.

In essence, the growth of digital nomadism paints a future in which cities and coworking spaces adapt to the rhythms of an international workforce that values freedom, flexibility, and sustainable living. As nomads, you're not just participants in this story—you're the very heartbeat, the pulse that keeps this vibrant system thriving. Remember, the cities of tomorrow are shaped by the choices you make today; by adopting this flexible, nomadic life, you're not just chasing dreams, you're building a future full of promise and unbound potential.

Economic and Environmental Considerations Imagine this: with a laptop slung over your shoulder and the zeal of a modern-day explorer, you're setting sail in the vast sea of digital nomadism. And as that dream crystallizes into reality, you're not just contemplating the thread count of your next AirBnB or the Wi-Fi speed at some exotic café; you're weighing the profound economic and environmental implications of your footloose lifestyle. Let's dive deep into what it means to tread that path with both fiscal savvy and eco-consciousness at the forefront of your mind.

First up: the economic perspective. When you unshackle yourself from a fixed location, you're doing much more than satisfying a wanderlust; you're engaging with a variety of economies, often in ways that traditional workers do not. This process can inject vitality into local markets through your expenditures on accommodation, co-working spaces, food, and cultural experiences. It turns out, your adventure also spins the wheels of local economies—a responsibility that comes with its own set of considerations.

Yet this impact is a double-edged sword. While your presence can be a boon to some, there's a nuanced conversation around the cost of living increases and gentrification that can be triggered by an influx of digital nomads. You see, as trendy neighborhoods brim with remote workers drawn by the siren call of Instagram-worthy backdrops, prices can skyrocket, and locals may be inadvertently priced out. Sensitivity to these economic shifts is paramount.

Switching gears, your role in the broader economic puzzle fits into the labor market dynamics. As a digital nomad, you contribute to a growing global workforce that's reshaping how businesses think about talent and employment. Your flexibility and diversity of experience can be a huge plus for companies looking to innovate and stay agile. You become part of a wave that promotes remote work as an economic model—championing work-life balance and, perhaps, a deeper, more fulfilling pursuit of professional satisfaction.

Now, let's paint with a broader environmental brush. Each flight you catch leaves behind a vapor trail of carbon emissions, and the more frequently you hop from one country to another, the larger your ecological footprint becomes. True, the wanderlust is an incredible feeling, but it comes bundled with an environmental cost that demands a moment's pause. Mitigating these impacts through choices like offsetting your carbon footprint or spending longer periods in each destination is a step towards reconciling your nomadic desires with planetary health.

Consider also the gear that accompanies you. Every new gadget represents a slice of the planet's resources converted into consumer electronics. As someone who may be more dependent on tech than most, the rate at which you consume and discard can become a reflection of sustainability—or the lack thereof. Opting for devices that last longer or choosing refurbished tech can become subtle, yet strong statements of your environmental ethic.

The minimalist lifestyle associated with digital nomadism has its green perks, too. With less space to fill and a greater awareness of the burden that possessions can be, you're likely to consume less 'stuff.' This reduction in consumer goods can alleviate some of the pressure we put on our environment, serving as an inadvertent nod to the 'reduce, reuse, recycle' adage. Sometimes, it's the things you don't buy that make the biggest difference.

And what about the relationships you build with your food? As a rolling stone gathering no moss, you've got the chance to indulge in local produce—seasonal fruits, vegetables, and other delights that haven't traveled thousands of miles to reach your plate. Supporting local agriculture not only provides you with fresh, nourishing fares but also helps cut down the food-miles that add to global emissions. The idea of 'eating locally' takes on a whole new hue when your local changes by the month.

Another fabric in the nomadic quilt pertains to energy usage. Co-working spaces and digital hubs around the world are increasingly wising up to green energy solutions, and your patronage can encourage further investment in this direction. By frequenting establishments that brag about their energy efficiency or renewable sources, you're reinforcing a market demand for environmentally-conscious facilities. Your choice of workspace becomes as much a statement as the work you produce within its walls.

Water conservation is a further touchpoint. The digital wanderer's life could mean shorter showers and less water-guzzling habits compared to the settled citizen with a lawn to sprinkle. It's about making conscientious choices even in the simplest acts, conscious of the precious droplets every region harbors. Being stingy with water resources, no matter where your travels take you, demonstrates a respect for the local ecosystem that won't go unnoticed.

Going beyond personal consumption, there's currency in the ideas you spread. As a digital nomad, you're a node in a global network, and the conversations you spark about sustainability can ripple through that network with surprising reach. Whether it's through blogging about green living or sharing eco-friendly travel hacks on social media, you wield influence. That smartphone in your hand is a gateway to encourage a community, whether transient or permanent, toward eco-friendly practices.

Don't underestimate, too, the economic boost you could provide to green businesses out there. Imagine the impact of consistently choosing accommodations that prioritize sustainability, or experiences that give back to the community rather than exploit it. Such spending sends a message that there's a market for responsible business practices, nudging other entrepreneurs to consider this path.

Let's not skirt around the fact that navigating these economic and environmental considerations can add layers to your decision-making. It might mean turning down that ultra-cheap flight in favor of one with a better carbon offset program or opting to fix your old device rather than buy the latest model. Every choice weaves into the tapestry of a future where digital nomadism doesn't just exist but thrives responsibly.

Tying all these threads together, you begin to see that being a digital nomad isn't just a personal journey; it's a collective adventure. You're not operating in a vacuum. Every border you cross, every transaction you make, every choice you execute—it's part of a living system where economy and environment are deeply entwined. Your mantra becomes a call for balance: seeking the riches of experience, while leaving the lightest of footprints. That's the noble harmony at the heart of your quest.

Let's wrap this with a nod to pragmatism. While it's great to champion planetary stewardship and economic empathy, don't forget the part where you need to make it all work practically. It's a juggling act—balancing the books of life in a manner that's not just sustainable for the world but also for you. After all, at the end of this path lies not just a sustainable world, but a life of profound and purposeful adventure for you, the digital nomad. Take that to heart, and every place you touch with your nomadic spirit will thank you for it.

Ethical Nomadism and Global Citizenship

Embarking on a nomadic lifestyle is more than a personal choice; it's a broader commitment to adaptability and responsibility in an interconnected world. Ethical nomadism stretches beyond the limits of just embracing remote work—it involves crafting a life that demonstrates respect for the cultures you immerse yourself in and fosters a global sense of citizenship. After all, being a digital nomad places you in a unique position to bridge gaps and embark upon life-changing interactions on a global scale.

Global citizenship might sound grand, but it isn't reserved for the philanthropists and peacekeepers alone. As digital nomads, we can form a mosaic of micro-contributions that resonate with the global citizen ethos. We are the new trailblazers, opting out of a sedentary lifestyle and choosing, instead, to learn from each new community and environment we encounter. Our travels are not only about the freedom to explore but also about the conscious choices we make along the way that affect local economies, environments, and societies.

Consider the local impact of your global footprint. Integration into diverse communities makes it imperative to create positive contributions, whether it's by supporting local businesses, engaging with local causes, or minimizing our environmental footprint through conscious travel habits. This is ethical nomadism in practice—ensuring that our presence adds value and doesn't extract value from the places we call temporary home.

Part of ethical nomadism is acknowledging that our work doesn't exist in a vacuum. As global citizens, digital nomads have the unique opportunity to collaborate across borders, cultures, and time zones. Our projects and interactions bring different perspectives together, championing inclusivity and innovation. This exchange of ideas doesn't merely enhance our work; it enriches our lives and broadens perspectives—this is the heart of global citizenship.

Moreover, economic considerations form an integral part of ethical nomadism. The money spent on accommodations, food, and experiences significantly impacts local economies. By choosing to stay in local guesthouses, dine at neighborhood eateries, and hire local guides, digital nomads contribute directly to the financial well-being of the communities they interact with. The ripple effects of these choices help sustain local traditions and foster economic growth.

It's crucial, however, to navigate this space mindfully. Being conscious of the fact that we are guests in a foreign land helps us approach each society with the humility and eagerness to learn that defines the essence of a global citizen. It's about respecting laws, customs, and rituals—even when they are vastly different from our own—and striving to leave no trace that would adversely change the cultural landscape.

Environmental stewardship also falls under the umbrella of ethical nomadism. Practicing sustainability—whether it's reducing plastic use, offsetting carbon emissions, or choosing eco-friendly transport options—demonstrates a commitment to preserving the world that we so eagerly explore. Global citizenship calls on us to protect the planet, not only for ourselves but for future generations of nomads and locals alike.

Becoming an ambassador for ethical practices isn't just beneficial for the areas nomads inhabit; it can also enhance personal growth. The principles of ethical nomadism encourage digital nomads to develop a deep sense of empathy and understanding, traits that are invaluable in both professional and personal realms. There's a profound satisfaction that comes from knowing your wanderlust isn't at odds with ethical considerations—it actually aligns with a more conscientious way of living and working.

Now, let's not overlook the challenge of balancing the nomadic lifestyle with ethical considerations. It's one thing to understand the importance of global citizenship; it's another to put it into consistent practice when easier, more convenient options are often at our fingertips. The digital nomad community plays a pivotal role here, sharing best practices, offering support, and holding each other accountable for the collective impact of our lifestyle.

Embracing digital nomadism also means embracing an ongoing education in global citizenship. Each new destination can be a classroom where learning isn't confined to books or lectures but lives in the daily interactions with new cultures and communities. Accepting that you are a perpetual student in this world can be a humbling and enlightening experience that forever shapes the contours of your character and the range of your empathy.

Connectivity is at the core of the digital nomad lifestyle, and it's more than just a technological convenience. It's a conduit to understanding, a way to break down barriers and foster a shared identity as inhabitants of this planet. Through our digital skills, we can promote messages of unity, collaborate on global projects, and connect with others who are driven to make a difference.

Treating ethical nomadism as a foundational philosophy rather than an optional add-on ensures that as we traverse the globe, we don't just pass through—we enhance, we enrich, and we empower. The digital nomad community is diverse, but we share a common thread: the desire for a life that is unbound and full of discovery. Let's commit to making sure that discovery is always coupled with respect and responsibility.

It's possible for the digital nomad movement to be a force for good, a testament to our ability to both witness the world and contribute to its welfare. Global citizenship isn't merely about having a good heart; it's about making choices that reflect that goodness, day in and day out, no matter where your laptop and luggage land next.

In the end, ethical nomadism isn't just a facet of the digital nomad lifestyle; it's a powerful way to wield the privilege of our flexibility and freedom. As we revel in the remarkable liberty to work from anywhere, let's strive to do so with purpose, with care, and with an unwavering commitment to our role as global citizens. Our nomadic journeys are not merely about us—they're about the mark we leave on the world and the kind of legacy that ripples far beyond our immediate horizon.

So carry your ethical compass along with your passport. Let it guide your way as you contribute to the tapestry of global citizenship, painting your journey with strokes of responsibility, empathy, and a deep appreciation for the diverse world you're exploring. With every step, understand that you are not only paving your own path but also shaping the path for those who follow. Ethical nomadism is the route to true global citizenship—a journey that we take together, forging a better world with every click of our keyboards and every stamp in our passports.

Chapter 10:
Future Trends in Digital Nomadism

The horizon of digital nomadism stretches far beyond today's co-working spaces and Wi-Fi hotspots. As we pivot to the future, it's thrilling to envisage how burgeoning technologies and shapeshifting market dynamics will sculpt the nomadic landscape. Imagine a world electrified by AI; its collaboration with human ingenuity creates possibilities where work seamlessly integrates with the wanderlust of the nomadic lifestyle. We're not just talking a fleeting trend—this is the dawn of an era where automation doesn't displace, but empowers the free-spirited entrepreneur.

Advancements in virtual reality could transport a designer from a sun-dappled beach in Bali straight to a client meeting in a virtual Manhattan high-rise, adding layers of efficiency and authenticity to remote interactions. With an eye on emerging hotspots, digital nomads might pivot to vibrant locales previously uncharted, ignited by local innovations and welcoming policies. At the heart of this upheaval is the expectation that tomorrow's workspace is not a fixed point on a map, but a continuum of experiences, unlocked by the digital keys we carry. These impending shifts are more than just simple iterations; they're quantum leaps that beckon us to leap before looking, to trust in the rapid current of change, ensuring that those who adapt with grace and foresight will write the next chapter of the digital nomad saga, a tale as untamed as the rolling vistas awaiting outside your future mobile office window.

Analyzing Market and Technological Trends

In the swirling cosmos of market flows and digital transformation, staying afloat means keeping your finger on the pulse of technological innovation and market shifts. As a future digital nomad, you've got to ride the wave of change, where AI is not just a buzzword but a steadfast ally in streamlining tasks and harnessing opportunities. You'll find that emerging tech, like decentralized currencies, widen paths to financial freedom and cross-border transactions. And keep an eye out for evolving job markets; they're already seeking remote savants skilled in cloud computing and digital marketing, hinting at the lush terrains of opportunity ahead. So, dive deep into these currents, for understanding the whims of technology and market trends is not just insightful, it's essential to thriving in a world that's constantly rewriting the rules of how, where, and when we work.

The Role of AI and Automation As we delve into the multifaceted world of digital nomadism, a groundbreaking shift is upon us, reshaping how we work and live. It's AI and automation – these aren't just buzzwords; they're the jet fuel propelling nomads into a stratosphere of opportunity. The savvy roamers amongst us have learned to harness these tools not as threats, but as allies in crafting a life of freedom and success on the road.

Consider the challenges of managing client relationships across time zones, or the intricacies of juggling projects while exploring the serenity of a Balinese rice terrace. AI steps in as your virtual sidekick, tackling tasks with precision while you're catching waves or catching up on sleep. From automated scheduling to AI-driven customer service bots, these technologies lift the burden of routine tasks, granting you more hours to immerse in your surroundings – or to simply indulge in the bliss of doing nothing at all.

Automation has dramatically altered the digital landscape in areas that directly benefit nomads. Think back to the hassle of accounting and invoicing – a necessary evil, right? Not anymore. With financial automation, not only do invoices get sent out with the click of a button, but they're also tracked, and payments are reconciled without breaking a sweat. It's as if you have a personal accountant in your backpack, one that doesn't take up space or demand a seat at the café table.

Let's chat about learning. To stay competitive, nomads must be lifelong learners, constantly upgrading skills. This is where AI comes in, offering personalized learning experiences that adapt to your pace and style. It's like having a mentor who's always on hand, offering insights and knowledge precisely when and where you need it. This constant companion allows for fluid personal growth, even as you hop from one continent to the next.

For those of us who thrive on crafting content, whether it's for a blog, social media, or client projects, automation tools for content creation can be a godsend. They churn out drafts, suggest edits, and even help with research. Sure, your voice is irreplaceable, but these tools act as the first mate in your creative journey, navigating through the roughest drafts to help you emerge with polished prose that resonates with your audience.

Project management is another realm where AI and automation shine for the digital nomad. Online tools visualize progress, track deliverables, and even predict timelines with machine learning. They're the oil in the gears of collaboration, ensuring no detail gets lost as you and your global team march towards success. It's almost like having a project management guru sprinkled across your devices, ensuring everything flows harmoniously.

As a digital nomad, you don't just get to explore the world; you also navigate the vast expanses of the internet. Here, AI-powered analytics tools play an essential role. They dissect website traffic, social media engagement, and ad performance, serving up valuable insights on a silver platter. By understanding what clicks with your audience, you're empowered to make data-driven decisions that propel your brand skyward.

Security, always a prime concern for the interconnected traveler, is bolstered by AI. From detecting fraud to securing transactions, AI acts as a guardian, a digital shepherd keeping your virtual flock safe. You can wander more freely, knowing that your online presence and assets are locked down tighter than a drum.

And let's not forget about networking. In this digital era, your network is your net worth. AI and automation simplify this by identifying potential connections, suggesting introductions, and even reminding you to follow up. It's high-tech schmoozing, but it expands your reach exponentially, connecting you with like-minded souls across the globe without requiring you to be glued to a screen.

Digital nomads often craft multiple income streams, and here AI opens doors to passive income. Automated digital storefronts, AI-curated stock portfolios, and property rental management tools generate revenue while nomads invest their time in passion projects or leisure. Imagine earning while you're hiking up Machu Picchu or diving in the Great Barrier Reef – it's not a dream but a real possibility through the smart use of automation.

But AI isn't just about logistics; it also touches the heart of your content. It can analyze emotional tone to suggest content tweaks for higher engagement, ensuring your message hits home every time. It's like a coach that's attuned not only to the words but also to the pulse of human emotion threaded through your digital tapestry.

For those apprehensive about the inevitable missteps along your journey, fear not. AI-powered tools offer a safety net, catching errors in real time, from typos in your emails to glitches in your code. It's a comforting layer of protection, giving you the confidence to leap into new projects knowing you have a digital safety harness.

As a nomad, staying fit and healthy is crucial, and yes, AI extends its reach here too. Fitness apps with AI tailor workouts for you, no matter where you set up your laptop. Nutrition trackers suggest meal plans based on local cuisine. It's wellness, personalized and portable, so you can maintain your health as you chase horizons.

To sum up, AI and automation are not the harbingers of an impersonal, sterile future. They are the enablers of a life rich with diversity and experience for the digital nomad. These tools liberate us from the tedium and unleash our potential in a world where the only constant is change. So, harness these allies, let them carry the load, and focus on what you do best – creating, exploring, living, and thriving in this boundless digital nomad landscape.

Embrace AI and automation as your partners on this thrilling odyssey. With them, you're not just keeping pace; you're setting the tempo for a symphony of experiences that will define your life as a digital nomad. Forge ahead with these smart tools, and let them pave the path to your extraordinary future, one where work and play are not at odds but in a harmonious dance guided by the rhythms of technology and human aspiration.

Emerging Destinations for Digital Nomads You've pieced together the puzzle of a nomadic life, embraced the tech, aligned your skills, and you're almost ready to cast away the conventional anchors. What's next? Finding the perfect spot that resonates with your spirit and your wallet. Beyond Bali, Bangkok, and Barcelona, there's a whole new wave of hotspots waiting to charm the ever-growing tribe of cyber wanderers.

Consider the pull of under-the-radar destinations—places where tourists trickle rather than flood. This is where the magic happens, where local life is palpable and your presence as a digital nomad can blend into the everyday rhythm. The cool thing? New spots are emerging through a blend of affordability, fast internet, and communities that capture the essence of global living.

Picture Canggu a few years back, a precursor reflecting the transformation that's underfoot in locations like Da Nang, where Vietnam's entrepreneurial spirit is as robust as its coffee. Fast Wi-Fi, exquisite cuisine, and an affordable cost of living are painting new pin drops on the map for digital nomads to explore.

Lest we forget, Latin America is simmering with potential. Medellín has been the poster child of nomadic renewal—its Paisa welcome, paired with a desirable climate, creates an irresistible draw. Yet eyes are turning to Santa Teresa in Costa Rica, where sunsets and surf coexist with coworking spaces nestled in jungle settings—a pure blend of work and play.

Europe isn't without its rising stars. Take Tbilisi, where ancient meets modern and your money stretches like the melted cheese in their famed Khachapuri. This Georgian gem offers a year-long visa for freelancers, making it not just a stopover but a place to stay and thrive.

Africa holds uncharted territories as well; spots like Taghazout mirror a Moroccan Canggu with its surf vibe and emerging digital community. It's not about the beaten path here, but rather the roads less traveled where your impact and experiences grow richer.

Each of these emerging destinations offers something unique: maybe lower costs, a supportive expat community, or an unrivaled connection to nature. Care to venture into a city revered for its art and music? Try out Leipzig, the new Berlin, with its own sort of gravitational pull for the creatively inclined.

Tallinn, with Estonia's pioneering digital infrastructure, welcomes remote workers with open arms. Its digital nomad visa program serves as an invitation to enjoy medieval charm alongside futuristic conveniences—a statement that nomad hubs aren't just tropical beaches but can also be cobblestoned and steeped in history.

Flip the compass to Asia once more, and there's Ipoh, Malaysia—affordable, rich in culture, and just the right kind of slow for those seeking a counterbalance to the frenetic pace of the more established hubs. Or consider Fukuoka in Japan, where the government's startup visa program entices global entrepreneurs, making it a promising base for innovation and exploration.

In South America, cities like Santiago, Chile, bring together incredible landscapes, a robust startup environment, and policies amenable to remote work. It's a confluence of factors making the city a strong contender for those seeking a blend of outdoor adventures and urban sophistication.

Let's not forget spots like Kraków, Poland—a European flavor without the Paris price tag. Kraków extends the promise of a cultural banquet and a burgeoning tech scene that favors the mobile workforce.

As you eye these emerging hotspots, consider their common thread: an increasing awareness that digital nomads are not just passing through. They're community builders, local economy boosters, and cultural bridges—attributes that shape the essence of nomadic living and inform the policies that welcome this new wave of global citizens.

Choosing your next destination is more than a pin on a map; it's a calculated leap into a lifestyle that transcends borders. Whether tucked away in an overlooked European city, a Latin American town pulsing with potential, or an Asian haven of serenity, there's a growing list of places hungry for the diversity and dynamism that you bring to the table.

The future is written in the footprints of those who dare to venture beyond what's known. As the landscape stretches to include more untapped regions, remember it's not just about chasing the conveniences but also contributing to the cultural tapestry and vibrancy of every place your journey takes you.

Embrace the uncertain and the undiscovered. Be pioneers in places where your lifestyle isn't just possible, but valued and cherished. There's a world out there reshaping itself to accommodate the freedom and fluidity of the digital age. It beckons with open doors—it's your turn to step through and become part of the narrative.

Anticipating Changes in the Digital Workspace

As digital nomads, we dance to the rhythm of an ever-changing technological beat, adapting our moves with every new innovation that reshapes the digital workspace. With the rise of digital nomadism, we've seen a dramatic shift from the traditional office to a world where the boundaries of our workplace are as fluid as our travel itineraries. But what's next on the horizon? Let's dive into the waves of change that are about to roll in.

We're steering into a future where the line between work and AI is blurring. Tools we currently consider cutting-edge will soon be as outdated as a flip phone in a 5G world. Tomorrow's nomad needs to stay one step ahead, ready to pivot with each technological advance, because it's not just about adopting new tools, it's about mastering them to work smarter, not harder.

Cloud computing isn't merely a convenience anymore; it's the beating heart of a nomad's office. Expect the cloud to become more intelligent, intuitive, and integrated into our daily tasks. It won't be long until real-time collaboration with team members from across the globe becomes as seamless as if we were sharing a desk.

But the digital workspace isn't just about tech upgrades. It's also about cultural shifts. Remote work has knocked down walls and connected us to a global talent pool. This diversity is a powerhouse of creativity, but only if you're prepared to embrace it. You need to become adept at working across cultures, time zones, and languages.

Privacy and security are also heading for a revolution. As nomads, we're susceptible to digital threats that could undermine our livelihood. Prepare to familiarize yourself with cybersecurity best practices, because when your office is as mobile as you are, guarding against cyber threats becomes as essential as locking your front door.

And as AI steps up to take on more mundane tasks, our roles will evolve. We'll shift from doing to managing and from task completion to creative problem solving. It means a potential for more freedom, but only for those who can adapt their skillsets to navigate an AI-assisted landscape.

Speaking of navigation, get ready for the era of 'smart workspaces'. Imagine entering a cafe and having your order, preferred workspace configuration, and ambient settings automatically adjusted because your personal AI has communicated with the cafe's system. That's the kind of personalization we can look forward to in the digital workspace.

Connectivity will see an uptick. With Starlink and similar services rising to prominence, the idea of a digital desert will become antiquated. As a result, expect less traveled paths to become hotspots for nomads seeking inspiration among untapped cultures and landscapes.

Now, let's talk about platforms. LinkedIn, Upwork, and their contemporaries may dominate today, but they'll evolve or be replaced by more dynamic, digital-nomad-focused networks. These platforms will not just facilitate job matches; they'll offer community support and learning resources tailored to the nomadic lifestyle.

Education and skill-building will be baked into the digital workspace. Microlearning platforms that enable you to pick up new skills on-the-go will be as common as coffee shops with free Wi-Fi. Continuous learning will be your ticket to staying relevant in a fast-paced digital market.

As digital nomads, the pull of wanderlust is strong, but so too should be our commitment to sustainable practices. The digital workspace will reflect a growing consciousness toward eco-friendly technologies and practices; it's on us to incorporate these into our nomadic lives.

Financial technology will see leaps forward as well. Cryptocurrency and blockchain are already changing the way we think about money and transactions on a global scale. Fasten your seat for a ride into a realm where decentralization isn't just a buzzword; it's the foundation of your financial transactions.

What about downtime? Virtual reality is closing in on a level of sophistication that may soon offer us a new way to unwind or network. Imagine VR co-working spaces where you can brainstorm with a colleague's avatar one minute and take a meditation break on a virtual beach the next.

Tapping into untouched markets will be a new frontier. Companies are discovering the value of remote workers who can introduce products to areas where traditional businesses have yet to venture. As a nomad, you've got the inside track to being the face and force behind these ventures.

Finally, anticipate a cultural shift in the perception of the digital workspace itself. Rather than a mere trend, digital nomadism is set to become a respected, sustainable way of life. We're not just participants in this movement; we're the pioneers shaping the future of work and redefining what it means to live and work in harmony with our passions and the world.

Stay eager, stay educated, and stay engaged with the world around you. The future is just over that next horizon, and as the digital workspace evolves, we must evolve with it. Remember, adaptability isn't just a trait; it's our superpower. Embrace it, and there's no limit to where we can go, or what we can do.

Chapter 11:
Living the Dream: Real-Life Stories

Now that we've navigated through the practical terrain of shaping your nomadic life, let's sprinkle some reality dust on our blueprint as we delve into the heartbeat of this adventure: the stories that stitch together the very fabric of digital nomadism. Narratives of those who've stepped boldly across the threshold of the conventional, to mould careers as boundless as their wanderlust, fill this chapter with technicolor experiences. These aren't just stories; they're modern-day odysseys showcasing grit, ingenuity, and the sheer exhilaration of living unconstrained by zip codes.

Mingled within these pages are tales of fearless freelancers who've scaled mountains while scaling their businesses, corporate escapees finding liberation in Balinese villas-turned-offices, and wandering souls who've carved out online empires between sips of chai in bustling marketplaces. Each anecdote brims with triumphs, tribulations, unexpected twists, and those serendipitous moments that seem almost scripted for cinema. Here is where you'll imbibe the essence of what it means to embrace digital nomadism not just as a lifestyle but as an art form, chiseling out a work-life symphony that resonates uniquely for each voyager. So, let's turn these stories into fuel for your own journey, as you edge ever closer to scripting your chapter in the great digital nomad narrative.

Inspirational Accounts from Seasoned Nomads

As you turn the pages of this narrative, discover the essence of a life unchained through the vivid anecdotes of those who've paved the asphalt with their well-worn soles—digital nomads that have transcended the conventional. These seasoned veterans of the road have summoned the courage to weather storms, dance with serendipity, and carve out sanctuaries in corners of the world most only see in glossy brochures. They share not merely the sunsets and skyline views but the grit and gusto it takes to rewrite the rulebook of work-life harmony. At the crossroads of wanderlust and Wi-Fi signals, their stories beat with the pulse of freedom, each a unique chord in the grand symphony of nomadic existence. Whether navigating the alleyways of ancient cities or finding tranquility on forgotten beaches, they've turned whispered dreams into tangible realities, proving that livelihood needn't be tied to a single zip code. Revel in their triumphs, absorb their wisdom, and let their journeys ignite the kindling of your own nomadic aspirations.

A Variety of Paths to Success Navigating the vast seas of digital nomadism, it's crucial to remember that there isn't just one charted course to reach the shores of success. Embarking on this lifestyle is akin to venturing into a labyrinth of endless corridors, each leading to different destinations yet all under the same enigmatic sky of remote work.

Some individuals dive headfirst into freelance writing or graphic design, carving out a niche by connecting with clients who value their unique blend of creativity and technical skill. Their success lies not just in their talents but their adaptability, learning to market themselves and manage projects from anywhere in the world. They embrace the liberty that comes with freelancing, picking projects aligned with their values and interests.

Then there are those who tap into the world of virtual assistance, organization, or data entry, supporting businesses and entrepreneurs with the precision and efficiency of a Swiss timepiece. These roles require diligence and exceptional communication skills, as well as a thorough understanding of digital tools to stay connected with clients across different time zones.

And let's not overlook the educators and coaches who transform knowledge into bridges, connecting learners to new skills and opportunities through online platforms. They create video courses, conduct webinars, or offer one-on-one sessions, simultaneously teaching and learning from the cultural exchange with a global audience.

For the tech-savvy, opportunities abound in software development, system administration, or cybersecurity. With companies ever more reliant on digital infrastructure, nomads with expertise in these fields are in demand. Success for them is a continuous journey of problem-solving and staying ahead of the curve in an ever-evolving technological landscape.

But success isn't reserved for those in the digital realm alone. Many digital nomads are entrepreneurs, establishing businesses that cater to fellow travelers or local markets. They find success by understanding the nuances of different cultures and consumer habits, blending innovative ideas with local flavors to create something truly special.

Others find an audience in content creation and social media, sharing their travels and lifestyle online, engaging followers with a blend of authenticity and aspiration. For these nomads, success is measured in likes, shares, and the ability to influence and inspire a digital generation.

Yet, regardless of the path taken, a common thread weaves through the lives of successful nomads: the mastery of balance—juggling the demands of work with the exploration and enjoyment of new destinations.

Project managers and scrum masters adapt their methodologies to a nomadic lifestyle, orchestrating symphonies of productivity from beachside cafes or mountain retreats. Success for these maestros comes from hitting targets and milestones while basking in the freedom of choice and location.

Seasoned professionals in fields like finance, consultancy, or law might opt to go remote, offering their expertise from anywhere they please. They leverage their years of experience, embracing telecommuting practices to offer high-quality advice while enjoying breathtaking backdrops.

For all the paths chosen, networking is as vital as ever; our nomads aren't isolated islands but rather nodes in a vibrant global network. Successful digital nomads actively engage in communities, both virtual and physical, fostering connections that can lead to new opportunities, collaborations, and friendships.

Of paramount importance is the ability to stay productive amidst distractions. Successful nomads create routines and rituals, crafting pockets of productivity within the fluidity of their travels. They recognize when to push through work and when to pause, soak in their surroundings, and find inspiration in the world around them.

Lest we forget, the path to success is also paved with personal development. Digital nomads often utilize their experiences to grow, not just professionally but personally. They reflect on their travels, learn new languages, pick up hobbies they encounter, and immerse themselves in each culture, thus enriching their work and worldview.

Success as a digital nomad is as diverse as the individuals themselves, each with their own definition and set of goals. For some, it's the accumulation of experiences, for others, financial stability, and for many, the freedom to structure their lives on their terms. In every case, it's the blend of passion, discipline, and flexibility that propels them forward.

In sum, success for a nomadic lifestyle hinges on one's ability to morph challenges into stepping stones. It's a path that includes continuous learning, adaptive strategies, and the courage to carve a personal and professional life that's as unique as a fingerprint – ever-changing, deeply personal, and universally human in its core pursuit of happiness and fulfillment.

The Highs and Lows of Nomadic Life Undeniably, embracing a nomadic lifestyle is akin to riding the crest of a wave. It's a journey punctuated by exhilarating highs and inevitable lows that test your resilience. Picture the mornings you'll wake up to mountain views, the clinking of your keyboard intertwined with the symphony of a bustling new city, the sense of achievement when landing a client from halfway across the globe. These moments capture the essence of the highs in our exploration of the digital nomad life.

Yet, let's not gloss over the moments that challenge our spirit. It's not all Instagram-worthy sunsets and trendy cafés. Connectivity woes, feelings of disconnection from loved ones, and the occasional pang of homesickness are some subdued notes in the nomadic melody. This life can oscillate between freedom and isolation, between discovery and the disquiet of the unknown.

Imagine the freedom to choose your office view, to die by the unwritten code of continuous travel, every corner of the world a potential home base for your restless soul. This is the heart-thumping exhilaration of casting off the bowlines, a promise of endless possibilities. You wake up to a new scene with every sunrise, your life a canvas of experiences painted with diverse cultures, cuisines, and conversations.

On the other hand, the low points can tug at your heartstrings with surprising strength. Financial instability can be a frequent, uninvited guest – never overstaying, hopefully, but its presence is felt. The fluctuating income is part of the package deal, one that can make you miss the predictable rhythm of a steady paycheck. This reality requires a blend of financial savvy and a stoic acceptance of leaner times.

Let's chat about community – or sometimes the lack thereof. Forging deep connections can be tough when you're always the new kid on the block. It's not impossible, mind you. It just demands effort, a willingness to put yourself out there, time and again. Digital nomads often find solace in fellow wandering souls and virtual communities, yet the absence of long-term neighbors and familiar baristas can weigh heavily.

Now, consider the freedom to set your own schedule. You're no longer a slave to the nine-to-five. Your time is yours to command. This flexibility allows for a work-life balance tailored to your desires, be it a morning spent exploring ancient ruins or an evening lost in work you're truly passionate about. It's an empowering aspect of the nomadic lifestyle that can skyrocket productivity and personal satisfaction.

Despite this, the downside to such autonomy can be a blurred line between work and leisure. The absence of traditional structure requires formidable self-discipline. Many nomads battle the temptation to slack in the face of tantalizing new distractions or, conversely, burn out while trying to keep pace with an always-on digital world.

Moreover, picture the personal growth that awaits. The nomadic lifestyle is a crucible, forging stronger characters through encounters with varied customs and the daily hustle of survival. You learn to be adaptable, creative, and resilient. Navigating foreign lands and languages teaches you more than any textbook ever could, not just about the world, but about the depths of your own tenacity and resourcefulness.

Yet self-doubt can be an unspoken struggle. The uncertainty of your next gig, the constant comparison to those seemingly flourishing back 'home,' can seed a sense of inadequacy. It's essential to anchor oneself in the knowledge that this journey is personal and that each step, whether forward or backward, is part of a grander narrative of growth.

Let's not overlook one of the purest highs: the sense of freedom. The digital nomad lifestyle gifts you wings to fly beyond the confines of conventional living. You quantify life in experiences, not possessions. You're light, not just in your suitcase but in your psyche, unburdened by the trappings of a stationary life.

But this lightness can come at the cost of stability. The transient nature of the nomadic life often leaves little room for roots to grow. Relationships can be fleeting, and there can be a yearning for regularity—a fixed gym membership, a local library, a go-to market. These fragments of a routine life can hold unexpected value when adrift in a sea of constant change.

Let's talk triumphs. When you land that client or nail a project against all odds, using makeshift workspaces and juggling time zones, you feel invincible. These victories are sweeter for their backdrop of uncertainty, a testament to your capabilities and a massive boost to your nomadic career credibility.

Conversely, consider the setbacks. Technical troubles in a town where no one speaks your language, or a missed flight wreaking havoc on an air-tight schedule. Such low points come with the territory. They're the messy reality of a lifestyle that trades security for adventure, and they teach you to be an unflappable problem-solver.

And then, there's the inexplicable joy of cross-cultural friendships that blossom in the most unexpected places. Bonds formed over shared meals, language barriers, and communal workspaces are unique treasures of nomadic life. These moments, where connections are forged in transient settings, make the heart swell and the world seem incomparably small and interconnected.

Contending with loneliness, however, is a common low. Isolated moments sneak up on you, times when the distance from your support network seems astronomical. It's in these instances that the digital nomad needs to summon their inner fortitude, to find solace in solitude, and remember why they chose this path.

Ultimately, the highs and lows of nomadic life are the ingredients of a unique, unrepeated recipe. Each digital nomad will savor different flavors, face distinct challenges, and seek their own balance in this lifestyle that blurs the lines of work, play, and life itself. It's a journey that is as rewarding as it is demanding, and if it calls to you, it's one worth exploring with courage and curiosity.

Chapter 12:
Crafting Your Legacy

While you've been traversing time zones, your work has been silently piecing together a mosaic of your existence—a legacy that spans the globe. Legacy isn't just about the money or the memoirs you leave behind; it's the digital footprint, the wave of influence and inspiration that echoes from your actions and work ethic. In the fabric of the internet, every blog post you pen, every project you launch, every cultural etiquette you adopt stitches a vibrant patch in the quilt of the digital nomad community. Crafting your legacy is about a conscious curation of your personal brand and online presence, a way to leave a mark while on the move that meshes seamlessly with the ebb and flow of global trends. It's about engaging with your audience, sharing not only your journey but your insights and growth, turning your experiences into a compass for others navigating this path. Your legacy isn't just for you; it's a beacon for those who will walk this road after you, a lighthouse of wisdom and wit shining across the virtual and geographic expanses that you've wandered. Remember, as you map out your virtual imprint, you're not just chronicling journeys—you're guiding futures.

Personal Branding and Online Presence

As you weave the threads of your nomadic tapestry, the power of personal branding and the art of crafting an online presence can't be understated. It's the digital handshake that introduces you to the world—a world that's increasingly remote and interconnected. Think of your online persona as your personal ambassador, one that travels at the speed of light across continents, bridging gaps and building connections. Whether you're a graphic designer with a penchant for minimalist aesthetics or a developer solving problems with elegantly written code, your online presence is the storefront of your professional life. Instagram, LinkedIn, your personal blog—these aren't just platforms; they're stages upon which you narrate your evolving story. And let's be clear: this isn't about vanity or soaking up likes. It's about planting seeds in the fertile soil of opportunity, tending to your personal brand with the same care and strategy as you would a business. Your goal? To create an authentic narrative that captivates and compels, turning followers into colleagues, and colleagues into friends. Forge your online presence with intention and creativity, because in the vast digital expanse, your legacy starts with a single click.

Leaving a Mark While on the Move can feel like trying to scribble your name in the sand just as the tide rolls in—constantly shifting, erasing, and challenging your presence. Yet, embrace this impermanence as a digital nomad, and you'll find it's not only possible to leave a lasting impression on the world, but also wholly necessary. Your legacy isn't just a byproduct of the work you do remotely; it's woven into the places you visit, the people you meet, and the stories you share.

A mark isn't always a physical thing. More often, it's the change you catalyze in a community or the inspiration you become for others dreaming of a similar path. Consider your journey an ongoing narrative—an opportunity to plant seeds of influence that might bloom long after you've packed up your laptop and moved to the next location.

Start with authenticity. Every Instagram post, every blog entry, every professional connection—they all carry the potential to resonate deeply with others. Share lessons learned, vistas captured, and personal growth achieved. Your unique voice is a beacon for kindred spirits, and in the vast digital expanse, being relatable creates ripples that can turn into waves of impact.

Imagine this: as you craft your professional narrative while hopping from continent to continent, each client or collaborator becomes part of your global network. They're not just business contacts; they're characters in your story, and you, in theirs. By working with integrity and leaving positive impressions, you weave patterns of goodwill that can surface opportunities in the most unexpected places and times.

Teaching and mentorship are potent tools for legacy building, too. Sharing your knowledge isn't just about creating blog posts or social media content—it's about taking the time to advise and support those who reach out. Whether it's through informal chats over coffee in a new city or structured webinars, those moments of guidance can be transformative for someone else. The value you give multiplies and extends your influence far and wide.

What about the footprints you leave in local communities? Supporting small businesses, participating in cultural exchanges, and volunteering—these actions intertwine your story with local narratives. When you invest time and energy into making a place better, even temporarily, you leave a part of yourself there. You're not just passing through; you're part of the community's history, however briefly.

On a broader scale, think about building your brand. Whether as a freelance designer, a developer, a writer, or any profession you hold, your brand is the sum total of your online presence, interactions, and work quality. Developing a brand that's synonymous with excellence and reliability, even as you move between time zones, solidifies your professional mark in your industry.

Pursue collaboration actively. Engage with other digital nomads, local entrepreneurs, and like-minded souls. Projects that allow you to cross-pollinate ideas with others not only enrich your own experience but often result in work that's innovative, impactful, and a testament to collaborative spirit. Such partnerships can lead to outcomes you would have never achieved solo, immortalizing your impact.

Diversification is also key. Your digital nomad journey should include a tapestry of projects and activities. This multidimensionality ensures that you're not just a one-note presence; you're a dynamic force engaging with the world in multifaceted ways. From creating art to building apps that solve real-world problems, each endeavor adds to your narrative.

Who could forget the simple act of storytelling? Document your travels, work, and experiences in a compelling way. These stories are not just for self-reference; they serve as beacons and guides for others who follow in your footsteps. Your anecdotes of overcoming obstacles, finding creative solutions, and navigating different cultures can become educational tools for future nomadic generations.

Take responsibility for the digital footprint you leave behind. Be conscious of the content you put out and its potential long-term effects. Positive, inspirational, and ethical content not only reflects well on you, but also inspires others and promotes goodness in the digital realm.

Use technology with intentionality. Tools that help manage your online presence, track your professional growth, and streamline your work processes aren't just for efficiency—they're for consistency. Regular engagement, updates, and management of your digital persona ensure that your virtual presence endures regardless of where your physical self might be.

Evolve constantly. The digital nomad landscape is one of perpetual change and those who adapt thrive. Keep learning, keep exploring, and keep pushing the boundaries of what is possible. As you grow, so does your potential to influence, and therefore, to leave an indelible mark.

Lastly, make giving back a non-negotiable aspect of your lifestyle. Whether it's through knowledge, time, or resources, the act of giving not only enhances the lives of others but also solidifies your legacy. It's the altruistic endeavors that truly define the depth of one's mark on the world.

To wrap it up, remember that the journey of a nomadic life is much like penning a novel where each place and interaction is a new chapter. Your legacy is defined by the narrative you create and the imprints you leave on the hearts and minds of people and places. So, as you glide from one adventure to the next, keep scribing your story with intention, ingenuity, and generosity, and you'll find your mark isn't just left in the sands of time—it's carved into the very essence of the nomadic spirit.

Engaging and Sharing Your Journey The sights are breathtaking, the tastes exotic, the experiences unforgettable. But your nomadic journey is more than the sum of its parts. It's a story, one that's begging to be shared. You're not just wandering the globe; you're crafting a narrative that has the power to inspire, connect, and resonate with others. Let's dig into the art of engagement, into the nuances of sharing our stories with the world while ensuring we're not simply sending messages into the void.

First, let's address the 'why'. Sharing your journey creates a bridge with your audience, be it friends, family, or a growing social media following. It's a nod to the human penchant for storytelling, an age-old tradition that brings us together, teaching us to dream and to learn from the experiences of others.

Expressing your adventures online is an exercise in authenticity. Documenting your lifestyle, work, places you visit, and the people you meet can provide valuable insights and inspiration for those contemplating a similar lifestyle switch. More importantly, it's not about curating a picture-perfect highlight reel; it's about being genuine and offering a realistic picture of what digital nomadism is all about.

Start a blog or a vlog, perhaps. This is your canvas. Here you can elaborate on your experiences with depth and personality, plus give useful tips and resources. Your blog could become a go-to for those aiming to follow in your footsteps. A vlog, on the other hand, makes it personal. Viewers can see your reactions, the landscapes you navigate—these visuals make your narrative visceral.

Engagement is a two-way street. Respond to comments, messages, and emails. Create a community around your content by being accessible, fostering discussions, and sharing your knowledge. Remember, the goal isn't just to showcase your life; it's to participate in an ongoing discourse, to learn, to give back.

Social media is your megaphone. Platforms like Instagram, Twitter, and Facebook can amplify your tales. Use stunning visuals on Instagram, quick updates on Twitter, and foster community discussions on Facebook. Each platform serves a unique function in shaping and sharing your digital nomadic journey.

But what about overexposure? Fear not. You can share intimately without sharing everything. Creating boundaries is healthy. It's possible to be open and captivate audiences while still protecting your personal space and private life.

Moreover, storytelling isn't just about where you are; it's about the journey. Share the setbacks and the comebacks—not just the success at the end of the struggle. Audiences resonate with vulnerability, with the hustle, the real talk about the ups and downs of living a life untethered.

Another key element is consistency. Like chapters of a novel, your shared content should flow. Regular updates provide structure to your story, making it easier for followers to stay engaged. Your consistent narrative thread helps you to build a sense of progression, and illustrates that growth isn't always linear—it zigs and zags and loops back on itself.

Diversify your content. Host Q&A sessions, write opinion pieces on nomadic trends, or collaborate with fellow nomads. Interviews with other travelers can offer new perspectives, and joint projects can expand your reach.

Remember, engage with other nomads too. Their stories and insights can enrich your own understanding, and those interactions build a network of peers that can be priceless both professionally and personally.

Another aspect of sharing your journey is utilizing it to further your career. As you document your path, you inadvertently create a portfolio that demonstrates your adaptability, problem-solving skills, and cultural sensitivity—assets that are invaluable in today's global marketplace.

So, what's the 'endgame'? Imagine a mosaic of experiences—a vibrant, complex picture of life on the road that encapsulates the essence of digital nomadism. This sharing is your legacy, a testament to a life lived boldly and creatively, a narrative that breathes with the spirit of exploration and connection.

Your journey is unique, and your story is yours alone to tell. Keep it vivid, keep it truthful, and let it echo in the digital expanse, a beacon for those yearning to break free and blaze their own trails. You're not just living the dream; you're passing the torch, igniting wanderlust, and sparking the courage for others to venture into the unknown, just as you did.

In sharing, you're not merely chronicling your exploits—you're birthing a community, creating a dialogue, and in some ways, you're subtly reshaping the narrative of work, life, and play. The world is vast, and yet, through your engaging tales, it becomes intricately interconnected—a grand network where each of us can find our place, our purpose, and our home.

Conclusion

In the tapestry of modern work-life, the threads of digital nomadism are woven with vibrant autonomy and resilience. As we've journeyed together through the chapters of this guide, a panoramic view of a lifestyle untethered from traditional constraints has emerged—an inviting horizon for those eager to fuse passion with wanderlust.

At the heart of digital nomadism lies the audacious spirit to redefine what it means to work and live. We've witnessed the crumbling of barriers once thought insurmountable, as technology and global connectivity forge new pathways for income and interaction. The nomadic mindset isn't just an adaptation; it's an evolution of consciousness, a bold step into personal freedom and professional fulfillment.

The tools that enable this lifestyle are as vital as the mindset that embraces them. The digital nomad's tech kit and fluency in leveraging online platforms aren't just conveniences; they're the lifelines that connect us to our work and to each other from any corner of the globe. Proficiency in these tools isn't a luxury—it's a necessity.

Setting out on your nomadic journey requires thoughtful planning and goal-setting, striking that delicate balance between the siren call of travels and the earthbound responsibilities of work. It's a dance of intricate steps—preparation meeting opportunity, with improvisation waiting in the wings.

As we build our remote careers, we embrace the ongoing negotiation between our current skills and the emerging demands of a digital landscape. Continuous learning is not just part of the journey—it's the fuel that propels us forward, expanding the vistas of opportunity and self-realization.

Mastering the logistics of nomadism, from negotiating legalities to navigating the nuances of financial planning, is nothing short of crafting your own safety net as you walk the high wire of global mobility. This agility is the hallmark of a successful digital nomad—one who meets complexity with creativity and challenge with courage.

And challenges will arise. Isolation, burnout, and uncertainty are as much a part of the nomadic narrative as the triumphs and breakthroughs. Yet in facing these setbacks, we don't merely endure; we transform. We cultivate resilience, deepen connections, and anchor our emotional wellbeing in a supportive community that spans continents.

A global mindset isn't just about embracing diversity; it's about threading the needle of cultural sensitivity with precision and respect. Our nomadic ventures are as much a journey inward as they are an expansion outward—each interaction, a chance to learn, to adapt, and to grow.

The impact of digital nomadism extends far beyond the individual. It's about the broader societal shifts, the reshaping of urban dynamics, and the ethical considerations that touch on environmental stewardship and global citizenship. The ripples we create as digital nomads can swell into waves of change, prompting us to ponder our legacy.

Future trends beckon with the allure of undiscovered terrain, inviting speculation and strategic thinking. The age of AI and automation may well redefine not just how we work, but also where and why. Staying attuned to these changes will enable us to not just navigate but anticipate the bends in the river of progress.

The real-life stories of fellow nomads serve as beacons, illuminating a spectrum of pathways each unique yet universally inspiring. Their lived experiences are a testament to the fact that while this lifestyle is neither simple nor easy, it is undeniably enriching—I dare say transformative.

Crafting your legacy, leaving your mark, sharing your journey—these are not mere footnotes in your nomadic narrative. They are chapters unto themselves, etching your presence into the collective memory of the global community and the virtual spaces we inhabit.

As we close the cover of this guide, let it not signify an end but a commencement. Armed with knowledge, insight, and resourcefulness, you stand at the threshold of possibility, ready to step into the embrace of a world without walls. Your journey is uniquely yours, but the roads that beckon are walked by many—a fellowship of nomads beneath a canopy of boundless sky.

The canvas of your future awaits your brushstrokes—bold, vibrant, and unabashedly yours. With every new sunrise in unfamiliar lands, with each connection forged across time zones, you are crafting a life rich with purpose and draped in the splendor of freedom.

So go forth, intrepid traveler of the digital age. Let the winds of curiosity billow your sails and the stars of innovation guide your course. The world is wide, the possibilities are limitless, and the journey is yours for the making. May it be as extraordinary as the vision that carries you onward.

Appendix A:
Resources for Digital Nomads

You've come a long way on your quest toward digital nomadism. You have unwrapped the layers of a nomadic mindset and dissected the essentials of a remote career. The transition, while thrilling, is dense with intricacies and requires a savvy set of tools and resources to implement it effectively. This appendix is designed as a compact go-to list for you, the soon-to-be world-wanderer with a laptop as your loyal companion.

Detailed List of Online Platforms and Tools

Embarking on this journey entails a sturdy bridge between your evolving skills and the opportunities the digital world offers. Thus, a curated list of online platforms and tools becomes your north star. Here, hyperlinks are your highways and profiles are your passports.

Remote Job Boards: Websites like FlexJobs, Remote.co, and We Work Remotely offer a plethora of job listings tailored for digital nomads seeking employment in various sectors. These are treasure troves for meaningful gigs.

Freelance Marketplaces: Platforms like Upwork, Freelancer, and Fiverr provide spaces for you to market your skills directly to clients. They're the perfect arenas to pitch, convince, and begin fruitful collaborations.

Professional Networking: For establishing connections that can lead to job opportunities, nothing beats LinkedIn. Tailor your profile to showcase your adaptability to remote work scenarios and the unique expertise you bring to the table.

Productivity Apps: Tools like Trello for project management, Slack for communication, and Evernote for note-taking are vital for keeping your workflow organized and maintaining efficient collaboration with teams, regardless of your time zone.

Travel Apps: Nomads need to navigate the physical world as smoothly as the digital one; platforms such as Skyscanner for flights, AirBnB for accommodations, and Rome2Rio for travel options become indispensable part of your toolkit.

These resources are just the tip of the iceberg. You'll discover more as you adapt and your needs evolve, but they serve as a strong foundation for starting out.

Guidelines for Remote Job Searches

The virtual job market is as dynamic as the waves of the ocean; hence mastering the art of searching is paramount. Here are some guidelines to get you sailing in the right direction:

Analyze the Job Descriptions: Look beyond the title. Understand the role's requirements, responsibilities, and company culture to determine if it's a match for you.

Craft a Tailored Application: Customize your resume and cover letter to speak to each opportunity. Highlight your adaptability to remote work and how your experience aligns with what they're looking for.

Be Proactive: Don't just rely on job postings. Reach out to companies you admire and pitch your value. Sometimes, opportunities are crafted through initiative, not just application.

Embrace Persistence: The competition can be fierce. Maintain a healthy balance between persistence and patience. Adapt your strategy as needed and keep learning from any feedback you receive.

Step by step, you'll find the combination that unlocks the door to your dream job. Use these resources and guidelines as a starting point, but always stay curious and eager to explore new possibilities. As you venture into the world, absorb its lessons, and when you find your rhythm, let your experiences empower others to pursue their own paths. This is the essence of digital nomadism—connecting, sharing, and thriving in a world without borders.

Detailed List of Online Platforms and Tools

Tapping into the right online platforms and tools is like finding your way to a hidden beach – once you're there, the horizon of opportunity stretches out infinitely. Let's delve into the virtual toolkits that can empower your nomadic life, starting with communication essentials. **Slack and Zoom** stand at the forefront, revolutionizing how we connect and collaborate with teams across oceans. They are the digital nomad's companions for brainstorming sessions while basking in the Bali sun or discussing deliverables amidst the bustle of a Tokyo coffee house.

There's more to being a digital nomad than just conference calls; there are the nuts and bolts of managing projects, and for this, look no further than platforms like **Trello** and **Asana**. They take the cake for organizing tasks and setting deadlines that align with your meandering time zones. You can map out your work schedule on the sands of time, or more precisely, on elegant boards and lists that represent your workflow.

But what about finding the work in the first place? **Upwork, Freelancer**, and **Toptal** are where you'll cast your net into the sea of freelance opportunities. These platforms are bustling markets of skill and demand, where writers, designers, developers, and more can find gigs aligned with their expertise. Think of them as your virtual resume, constantly connecting you to potential clients while you enjoy that fresh coconut by the Mediterranean.

While we're harnessing technology to bring our work anywhere, let's not forget the essentials of getting paid. Enter **PayPal, TransferWise** (now known as **Wise**), and **Stripe**: the holy trinity of managing finances across borders. With these in your arsenal, handling invoices, payments, and international transfers becomes as seamless as the transition from mountain vistas to urban landscapes.

Learning and upskilling are non-negotiable for the thriving nomad, and platforms like **Coursera, Skillshare**, and **Udemy** offer an ocean of knowledge at your fingertips. These are the wellsprings of new knowledge, allowing you to dive into anything from programming languages to digital marketing, ensuring your skills stay as fresh as the local cuisine you're feasting on.

And then there's the hunt for that perfect spot to set up your laptop. **Coworker.com** and **Workfrom** are like compasses pointing you to the nearest coworking spaces, complete with reviews and amenities, ensuring you have the perfect blend of community and connectivity as you navigate new terrains.

Let's not forget our wanderlust. When you're in search of your next temporary abode, platforms like **Airbnb** and **Booking.com** are akin to trusty map scrolls, revealing a myriad of accommodation options. Whether it's a cosy loft in Prague or a beach villa in Costa Rica, these sites help you find the ideal haven that complements your nomadic life.

Data security should be a paramount concern, too. Applications like **LastPass** and **1Password** act as digital vaults, safeguarding your passwords like the guardians of a fortress, while VPN services such as **NordVPN** and **ExpressVPN** serve as cloaks of invisibility to protect your online maneuvers from prying eyes in public networks.

Being productive on the go means having a slew of apps that bring your office with you. **Google Suite** and **Microsoft Office 365** are the alphabets and syntax of the nomad's language, enabling the creation of documents, spreadsheets, and presentations. They make sure your office is as mobile as you are, allowing for real-time collaboration and updates no matter where you find yourself.

Digital nomadism isn't all work; it's about the lifestyle, too. Platforms like **Meetup** and **Eventbrite** are your tickets to local events, workshops, and seminars. These tools allow you to merge into the social fabric of your temporary homes, ensuring your journey is rich with connections and experiences that extend beyond pixelated screens.

Health is wealth, especially on the road, and apps like **Headspace** and **7 Minute Workout** keep your mind and body in check. They remind you to take care of your well-being, providing you with mental breaks and physical routines that can be done in the comfort of your Airbnb or between flights.

Lastly, staying organized and on schedule is imperative. Calendar apps like **Google Calendar** and **Apple Calendar** are the metronomes of your nomadic symphony. They ensure you dance to the rhythm of deadlines and meetings while still allowing plenty of time for improvisation and exploration.

Every tool mentioned here plays a crucial role in weaving the tapestry of a digital nomad's life, with each thread and color representing different facets and needs. But remember, the true magic doesn't lie solely in the tools themselves but in how you wield them amidst the ever-changing backdrop of your travels.

Empower yourself with these instruments of digital wizardry and watch how they transform your work, learning, and connections. Imagine never missing a beat in your professional life, even as the scenery shifts from metropolitan marvels to tranquil tropics. With this toolbox, you're not just working remotely – you're redefining the very essence of freedom and productivity.

So pack these digital tools along with your passport, charger, and an open heart. As you venture into the world of digital nomadism, they are the companions that will help you navigate, thrive, and ultimately, transcend the ordinary confines of a desk-bound job. They will be your bridge to the world, allowing you to savor the planet's vastness while you carve out your unique mark in the digital universe.

Guidelines for Remote Job Searches

Finding a job that allows you to zip across time zones and work from your desired corner of the world requires a certain finesse. It's a twirling dance between showcasing your skills and understanding the rhythms of the remote job marketplace. Let's unfold some key steps to refining your remote job hunt—an odyssey worth every bit of sweat and late-night coffee.

Before jumping in, let's get one thing straight: remote job searching isn't a mere click-and-apply routine. It's a strategic quest for that golden opportunity which meshes well with your wanderlust lifestyle. Remember, it's about quality over quantity. Target your job search on positions that resonate deeply with your skills and alignment to digital nomadism.

Revamp your resume to reflect your self-discipline, adaptability, and experience with remote work—even if it's just that time you collaborated online for a university project or managed a task while traveling. Highlight your communication skills, time management prowess, and familiarity with digital productivity tools. This isn't about inflating your experience; it's about showcasing what you bring to a virtual table.

Utilize job platforms that cater to remote work like We Work Remotely, Remote.co, and FlexJobs. These are treasure troves filled with opportunities that suit the digital nomad lifestyle. However, don't overlook general platforms like LinkedIn. Often, companies list remote positions there citing 'location independent' or similar phrases in the job description.

Networking is not just a buzzword; it's essential artillery in your job-hunting arsenal. Reach out to fellow nomads on forums, LinkedIn, and social media groups specific to digital nomads. Often job leads and opportunities are shared within these circles before hitting mainstream job boards.

When you're applying, your cover letter should sing the tune of a digital nomad—reliability, independence, and resourcefulness. Paint a picture that allows potential employers to visualize you thriving in an untethered environment. And yes, they should feel confident that you understand Wi-Fi is as vital to you as water—metaphorically speaking.

Prepare for interviews with an emphasis on your ability to work autonomously. Employers need to feel assured that you won't crumble when faced with spotty internet or a twelve-hour time difference. Show them you've got a toolkit to combat these challenges, and boomerang back with resilience and problem-solving skills.

Once you land that interview, remember the mantra: Professionalism doesn't imply being unheard in a coffee shop. Find a quiet, well-lit space, test your tech, and ensure a strong internet connection. Your first impression in an interview should echo the qualities expected of an exemplary digital nomad.

An often-overlooked step in the remote job hunt is to analyze the company's culture and their approach towards remote work. Does the organization have a remote-first ethos? Or are they dipping their toes into the remote world for the first time? Understanding their stance can provide significant insight into how seamless your experience will be.

Be clear about your needs as well: Do you prefer synchronous or asynchronous communication? Are you looking for flexible hours or a fixed schedule? Discuss these nuances during the interview to ensure alignment with the potential employer's expectations.

Always negotiate with the knowledge of the financial implications of digital nomadism. Factor in costs like travel, insurance, and co-working spaces when considering your salary requirements. Be transparent about these necessities when the talk of compensation arises.

Once you secure a position, it's fundamental to initiate a system that supports your nomadic workflow. Establish daily rituals, set clear boundaries, and maintain regular check-ins with your team. The idea is to forge a structure that travels with you, ensuring continuity in productivity and engagement.

While on the subject of continuity, remember to perceive job search and skill development as ongoing tasks. Your next remote role could arise from a new skill learned today. Stay curious, learn continuously, and keep your digital toolbelt ever-evolving. The digital nomad job market is constantly shifting—make it a point to shift with it.

And when uncertainty creeps in during your search—because let's face it, at times it will—draw upon the larger picture. Each application sent, each network connection made, and every interview attended brings you a step closer to blending work with wanderlust. Charge onward with the knowledge that resilience in the search mirrors the resilience needed on the road.

In summary, your remote job search should be as nimble and dynamic as the lifestyle you're aspiring to live. Tailor your approach, reinforce your skills, connect fervently and negotiate mindfully. The digital nomad's career is not just about living in the moment but creating it, one application, one conversation, and one remote gig at a time. Here's to finding your perfect match in the vast expanse of remote work possibilities!

Appendix B:
Pre-Departure Checklist

So, you've threaded the needle of preparation, winding your way through the why's, the how's, and finally stepping closer to the grand embrace of digital nomadism. It's a cusp moment—an interlude between the dream and the journey. And now, before you leap into this globe-trotting adventure, it's time to ensure nothing vital gets left behind. This pre-departure checklist is your trusty sidekick, making sure you're geared up, ready to roll, and have all your bases covered.

Essential Steps Before Embarking on Your Nomadic Adventure

Review Your Goals and Itinerary

Pin your personal and professional targets to the board once more. Realign them with the destinations on your itinerary to maximize both work productivity and explorative thrills.

Finalize Legal Documents

Your passport should have plenty of blank pages and be valid far beyond your return date. Visas, insurance policies, and other legal documents need to be double-checked and securely stored—both physically and digitally.

Financial Housekeeping

Ensure your banking needs are in order, be it setting up international accounts, notifying your bank of travel plans, or making sure you know the exchange rates and fees you're working with.

Health Comes First

Get all necessary vaccinations, and stock your first-aid kit. Also, remember to have a digital copy of your medical records and prescription scripts, and to research healthcare options in your destination.

The Digital Nomad's Tech Check

Confirm that your tech arsenal—laptop, smartphone, chargers, adapters, and backup drives—are in working order. Wi-Fi boosters or a reliable hotspot can save the day in connectivity deserts.

Communication Setup

Plan how you'll stay in touch with clients, colleagues, and loved ones. Whether it's a comprehensive calling plan or a stable internet setup for video conferencing, smooth communication is key.

Your Virtual Base

Set up a virtual mailbox, cloud storage for necessary documents, and any other online services that will act as your digital anchor.

Packing Like a Pro

Curate a sleek, versatile wardrobe and gear selection that goes the distance. Multi-purpose items save space and schlep. And don't forget those creature comforts that transform any place into 'home'.

Accommodation Arrangements

Secure an initial stay and plan for flexible future bookings. Remember to read reviews and confirm the Wi-Fi quality—for you, it's about more than just a comfy bed.

Say Goodbyes... for Now

Have a proper send-off with friends and family. Remind them this isn't farewell, but a 'see you on the flip side'—with a trove of stories en route.

The wind's at your back, the digital highway awaits, and adventure beckons with a siren call. This checklist is your passport to peace of mind, a pact with yourself to be as ready as one can be for the unfolding odyssey. With every item ticked off, you're liberated to ride the wave of change, soak in the sunsets, and nurture the seeds of your ambition in the fertile soil of the world. There's a skyline out there waiting for your silhouette. Onward, nomad.

Essential Steps Before Embarking on Your Nomadic Adventure

Before you cast off the bowlines and dive into the invigorating world of digital nomadism, there's a tapestry of tasks to tackle. Mapping out your journey is about more than pinning destinations on a globe; it's about threading the needle between your current life and the nomadic dream with precision and care.

Step 1: Assess Your Current Situation

Begin by taking a hard look at where you stand. This means reviewing your financial health, existing job situation, personal relationships, and assessing what changes need to be made. An exit strategy is vital; plan how to transition from your current living arrangement to a life of mobility without leaving chaos in your wake.

Step 2: Get Your Finances in Order

Money talks in every corner of the world, and for a digital nomad, financial stability is key. Start by setting up a robust budget plan that accounts for travel costs, daily expenses, and emergencies. Explore international banking or find financial services that cater to nomads to avoid exorbitant fees.

Step 3: Downsize and Declutter

The art of letting go applies to possessions as much as it does to outdated notions of work. Embarking on a nomadic lifestyle often means downsizing your belongings to the essentials. Sell, donate or store your surplus stuff. Simplicity is liberating and practical when you're globe-trotting.

Step 4: Secure a Remote Income

Unless you've got a hefty nest egg, you'll need a steady stream of income. Fortify your existing job for remote work or pivot towards new opportunities in the digital market. Ensure your income source is reliable and resilient to the shifting tides of travel.

Step 5: Upgrade Your Skills

Never underestimate the power of continuous learning. Whether it's mastering a new digital tool or polishing your language skills, equip yourself with shiny new assets that enhance your nomadic life and work.

Step 6: Go Digital with Documentation

Important documents should travel with you, not just in your backpack, but in the cloud. Keep digital copies of all critical paperwork such as passport, ID, insurance policies, and health records, accessible and secure.

Step 7: Research and Plan Your Destinations

Dream destinations aren't just about the Instagram shots; they're about the cost of living, internet reliability, and the local community. Thorough research will prevent you from landing in a paradise plagued with impracticalities for work.

Step 8: Network, Network, Network

Digital nomadism blossoms with connections. Reach out to other nomads, join online forums, and become part of the global community. The insights and friendships you gain are invaluable.

Step 9: Health and Travel Insurance

Healthcare is a universal concern, especially when your address zips across time zones. Secure insurance that keeps you covered globally and gives peace of mind, so you can focus on your adventures.

Step 10: Establish a Routine

Even amid the freedom of nomad life, a routine grounds you. Outline a realistic daily schedule that balances work and exploration. Adaptability is key, but a semblance of structure will keep you productive.

Step 11: Tackle Language Barriers

Learning the basics of the local language not only smooths your daily interactions but also enriches your cultural experience. It's a gesture of respect that opens more doors than you might expect.

Step 12: Prepare for the Unexpected

Even the best-laid plans can go awry. Have a contingency plan for when things take an unexpected turn. This might mean setting aside an emergency fund or having backup plans for accommodation and travel.

Step 13: Embrace Minimalism

In both possessions and lifestyle, minimalism can be a superpower. It allows you to swiftly adapt, move and find joy in experiences over things. Plus, packing is a breeze when you live by 'less is more'.

Step 14: Set Your Communication Strategy

How will you stay connected with loved ones or clients across multiple time zones? Determine the tools and apps that work best for you and schedule regular check-ins to nurture relationships back home.

As you stand on the precipice of change, these steps aren't just tasks to check off; they are the starting chords of your nomadic symphony. A smooth beginning begets a harmonious journey, and with every step forward, you knit the rich tapestry of a life woven with freedom, adventure, and purpose. So, stitch these essential steps firmly into the fabric of your planning, and watch as the world becomes your backyard, office, and home.

www.ingramcontent.com/pod-product-compliance
Lightning Source LLC
Chambersburg PA
CBHW051245050326
40689CB00007B/1075